SHAME ∾ SCHAM

a collaboration

Robert Kelly ∾ Birgit Kempker

birgit kempker

Robert Kelly

Of 400 signed copies this is number __*153*__

SHAME~SCHAM

SCHAM~SHAME
KELLY~KEMPKER

KEMPKER~KELLY

MCPHERSON & COMPANY

SHAME / SCHAM

a collaboration by Robert Kelly and Birgit Kempker

Copyright © 2004 Urs Engeler Editor, Wien and Basel, Weil am Rhein.
Special contents of this edition copyright © 2005 McPherson & Company.

Published by McPherson & Company
Post Office Box 1126, Kingston, New York 12402
www.mcphersonco.com
Publication of this book has been made possible by
the Literature Program of the New York State Council on the Arts.
Manufactured in the Czech Republic by Finidr.
Typeset in Minion. Printed on pH neutral paper.
Title page spread designed, printed and tipped
at McPherson & Company.
First U. S. Edition
December 2005

Library of Congress Cataloging-in-Publication Data

Kempker, Birgit, 1956-
  [Scham. English & German]
  Shame/Scham / Kelly/Kempker = Scham/shame / Kempker/Kelly.
    p. cm.
  English and German.
  "A collaboration by Robert Kelly and Birgit Kempker."
  ISBN 0-929701-77-1 (alk. paper)
  I. Kelly, Robert, 1935-   II. Title: Scham/shame. III. Title.
PT2671.E429S3313 2005
831'.914—dc22

                            2005027375

Publisher's Note

Shame/Scham is a bilingual sequence by Birgit Kempker (German) and Robert Kelly (English) in sixteen alternating exchanges. It was constructed between November 2001 and August 2004. Kempker and Kelly used e-mail exclusively, and did not meet or speak throughout the whole period—the entire contact was through, and in response to, the sections of the sequence itself as they were written and sent to the other. The text is always responding to itself. Another chosen constraint was that each poet had to write at least one passage in each section using the language of the other.

As published in this book, the original texts as composed are printed on the right hand pages, and the translations face them on the left hand pages.

As the composition neared its completion, the German editor Urs Engeler (publisher of the European edition of this book) proposed that each of the authors translate the work of the other. As a consequence, the complete work may be read entirely in English, entirely in German, entirely in the original, entirely in translation, or in any admixture —and always the language the reader encounters is the authentic language of one of the authors.

In every case the right hand page is the original text, the left hand page is its translation. Passages enclosed in // // were composed by the translator—they are riffs or asides added in the act of translation. The occasional brief German passages appearing originally in Kelly's texts are taken over entire in Kempker's corresponding translations; English translations for these pieces are provided on pages 238-40. Note too that the two poems beginning on pages 188-89 in #13, for and against Rilke, were composed in a criss-cross way: Kempker wrote her attack in English, Kelly wrote his praise in German. (An English translation of Kelly's poem is to be found on page 239.)

3

SHAME 1

I put the spell on you is the sentence about shame that I hear.
I hear: *Not the same,* knot the seed, semen. Notate the name.
I thought a spell was what the body spits between
somebody's legs. The skull cracks in the fire, oracle bone.
The bush of the body branches out at the other end along
the Ganges. The soul climbs. The schoolboy holds his hand,
long ago grown numb, up in the air forever. // *He seems to
ask. To leave this room. To answer the question.* // His hand
holds his promise. His fingernails curl around his arm.
Malice is a flower evacuated on the body. Many such flowers
blossom in great remoteness from the action. Blossom is
translation from spelling. Reading means: to make room
for fear. The flourishing of wounds attracts jackals. Among
people, if I want to feel attracted to somebody, I try to make
them feel shame. The shame when I confront myself is the
shame when I confront my soul. The soul is an invention to
keep me from feeling ashamed of my death.

SCHAM 2

Eine Schande bin ich, so lange brauchte, brauche ich, endlich
zu antworten. In meinem Schweigen und Verzögern steigt die
Blasphemie des Wortes auf. Das Wort in diesem Fall ist
Scham. *Shame bedeutet Scham, doch sham bedeutet falsch. Ich
bin falsch. Scham und Schuld, man muss unterscheiden, nein,
entscheiden.* Ein Mann muss seine Scham aus der Scheide
ziehen.

SCHAM 1

I put the spell on you ist der Satz zu Scham, den ich höre. Ich höre: Not the same. Knote den Samen. Notiere den Namen. Ich dachte, spell sei Spucke und zwischen die Beine. Der Schädel knackt im Feuer. Es spaltet sich der Busch des Körpers am anderen Ende darin am Ganges. Die Seele steigt. Der Schüler hält die abgestorbene Hand für immer in die Luft. Die Hand hält sein Versprechen. Die Fingernägel umranken den Arm. Das Schandmal ist eine ausgelagerte Blume am Körper. Manche solche Blumen blühen in großer Entfernung zur Tat. Blühen ist Übersetzen von Buchstabieren. Lesen ist, die Furcht beherbergen. Doch das Florieren der Wunden zieht Schakale an. Ich gestehe, dann wen zum Schämen zu bringen, wenn ich mich angezogen fühlen möchte zwischen Menschen. Die Scham vor mir selbst ist die vor meiner Seele. Die Seele ist eine Erfindung, damit ich mich für meinen Tod nicht schäme.

SHAME 2

Eine Schande bin ich, it took me, takes me, so long to answer. In my silence and delay rises the blasphemy of the word. The word in this case is shame. Shame bedeutet Scham, doch sham bedeutet falsch. Ich bin falsch. Scham und Schuld, man muss unterscheiden, nein, entscheiden. A man has to unsheathe his shame.

Jetzt weiss ich es. Die Schamteile, wie sie die alten Bücher nennen, die Scham selbst aus ihrer schamvollen Scheide gezogen. Wir Leute mögen uns nicht wirklich gegenseitig. Wir machen, dass Teile von uns in Teile von anderen Leuten passen, mögen es, wie es sich anfühlt, und hassen, dass es passieren muss. Kein Wunder nennen wir sie Schamteile.

Wir hassen es, Gefühle zu haben, denke ich. Alle Gefühle können zu anderen Gefühlen führen, Schmerz zum Beispiel. Tibetanische ngag-pas beobachten, wie die Geier den armen alten toten Mann säuberlich verspachteln, und nun liegt er da gebrochen auf den Felsen. Der ngag-pa übt sein Ritual aus, bietet sich selbst mit dem Fleisch des alten Mannes, rührt mit seiner Hand die grosse Trommel: der Geierzirkel. Vielleicht will er Freiheit von seinen Gefühlen. Man nennt das: Schneiden. Cutting.

Sind wir nicht beschämt, genauso beschämt, Gefühle zu haben? Ein Mann erblickt eine Frau mit Begierde, und sein Freund sagt O, du magst sie? und der Mann schämt sich, seine Begierden sind aufgedeckt. Es ist töricht, Gefühle zu haben. Es ist eine Schande, irgendwas zu fühlen.

Nun ist es Zeit, mit den Wölfen zu heulen. Meine Begierden sind aufgedeckt. Mein Wille ist nackt und ich muss schreien, um dich von meinem Schweigen loszuschneiden.

Now I know. The parts of shame the old books call them, the shame itself unsheathed from its shameful scabbard. We, people, do not really like each other. We make parts of ourselves fit together with parts of other people, and we like how it feels but we hate that it has to happen. No wonder we call it parts of shame.

I think we hate it that we have feelings. All feelings can lead to other feelings, pain, for instance. Tibetan ngag-pas watch vultures feasting neatly upon some poor man dead of pneumonia now stretched out broken on the rocks. The ngag-pa does his ceremony, offering himself along with the meat of the dead man, he throbs his big hand drum, the vultures circle. Maybe he wants freedom from his feelings. This is called Cutting.

Aren't we ashamed, also ashamed, to have feelings? A man gazes at a woman with desire, and his friend says O, you like her? and the man feels ashamed, his desire has been discovered. It is foolish to have feelings. It is a shame to feel anything.

But now it is time to howl. My desires have been uncovered. My will is naked. I have to scream to distract you from my silence.

Yesterday I was ashamed of my reaction to a white rose. I am ashamed that I drink milk, when I sit and think about milk, and add some honey, because of the tenderness of something out there in the garden, and my own head feels faint and I just want to yield. That doesn't work. I'm not completely born yet. I know that. When I wept because of the rose or when my pencil was writing: When I wept because of the rose, I felt like a friend who writes to me: I cried again. Another one writes: Later we will live beside one another just like plants. I am ashamed to tell that falsely, to be a lying witness.

I am ashamed of these kinds of love that don't count in life. I'm ashamed of my way of always counting. I am ashamed of my hands, through them, what was supposed to be mine, just runs away. I am doubly twisted around and stitched down in the wrong place. I am ashamed of being bashful, keeping my desires hidden and not catching fire, or keeping everything in futility, far away from me. When bashful people are shameless, it thrills me. I love courage. I fear my own. I lollop around the field of love.

An unloved body should be ashamed, a body that stays hidden and keeps putting off the times to blossom, times that pass away and the chance is lost. Shame hides. Hairs are hormonal signs. Love works wonders for the hair-do, taken along with sexual activity. Your hair is uncontrollable, he'll

Gestern schämte ich mich für meine Reaktion auf eine weisse Rose. Ich schäme mich, dass ich Milch trinke, wenn ich über Milch nachdenke und Honig hinzufüge wegen der Sanftheit von etwas draussen im Garten und in meinem eigenen Kopf hinfällig werde, mich abgeben will. Das geht nicht. Ich bin nicht zu Ende geboren. Ich weiss das. Als ich wegen der Rose weinte oder als mein Bleistift schrieb: Als ich wegen der Rose weinte, fühlte ich mich wie ein Freund, der mir schreibt: Ich weinte schon wieder. Ein anderer schrieb: Wir werden später als Pflanzen nebeneinander leben. Ich schäme mich, das falsch zu sagen, ein Lügenzeuge zu sein.

Ich schäme mich für diese Arten von Liebe, die im Leben nicht zählen. Ich schäme mich für meine Art des Zählens. Ich schäme mich für meine Hände, durch die, was für mich ist, weg rinnt. Ich bin doppelt verkehrt verdreht immer an der falschen Stelle zugenäht. Ich schäme mich, dass ich schamhaft bin, Begierde nicht zeige und nicht entzünde, oder in grosser Vergeblichkeit und Entfernung von mir. Wenn Schamhafte schamlos sind, bin ich hingerissen. Ich liebe Mut. Ich fürchte meinen. Ich hoppel im Liebesfeld.

Ein ungeliebter Körper soll sich schämen, der verborgen bleibt und es versäumt, die Male zu blühen, die eingeräumt sind, und die Frist vergeht. Scham kaschiert. Haare sind hormonelle Zeichen. Liebe wirkt Wunder auf die Frisur in Einheit mit sexuellen Tätigkeiten. Dein Haar ist unregierbar,

say, your hair is wild and gleaming all through London, the wild man will say: *Your hairs look such nice, lady*, and then it's all over. They look at me with eyes full, till they close their eyes and get me inside, they're full, they want to let me go forever, they ate me up, and I'm ashamed to be let go of. Why is it that not being there is what I can do for you?

I hate feelings. Feelings hurt. Naturally it's not pretty to write "I'm ashamed." Maybe a little pretty. Earlier I was ashamed of the word "silence!" Silence, significance, promises. False feelings are nauseating. True even more so. But there are no false feelings. Feelings are false. They change in no time. They reverse suddenly. They wobble. They even stop abruptly. You sit across from me. I button up my jacket. The waiter brings the candle. He is from Berlin, Charlottenburg. You see my blue halter. Cornflower blue. I've wanted to show it. I've waited for someone to say: Pull it tight. I pull it tight. I show my breast, quickly, lightly, like a robin that will be soon struck down, then I button up my jacket. You say: I love you. You pull up your sweater and show your shirt. The breast. Slow, slower than I show my halter. This moment, I've waited for it all my life. Quick, tender, full of recognition, beautiful and cautiously brave, using the power set free. Then you say: It's no good. I say too quickly: But it's beautiful, you take my hand, you say that your love is too small and that you don't want to be my man and you don't want to have me as your wife, the woman you have and had from the beginning, you don't want to live with me. On account of the flow. You flow with

wird er sagen, du wirst es leuchtend durch London tragen, der wilde Mensch wird sagen: Your hairs look such nice, lady, und dann ist alles vorbei. Sie sehen sich die Augen satt an mir, bis sie diese schliessen und mich erfassen, satt sind, um mich für immer zu lassen, die frassen, dafür schäme ich mich, losgelassen zu sein. Warum ist es das, was ich für dich tun kann, nicht da sein?

Ich hasse Gefühle. Gefühle tun weh. Natürlich ist es nicht schön «ich schäme mich» zu schreiben. Ein bisschen schön schon. Früher schämte ich mich für das Wort «Schweigen». Silence, Bedeutung, Versprechen. Falsche Gefühle sind eklig. Echte erst recht. Es gibt aber keine falschen Gefühle. Gefühle sind falsch. Sie ändern sich sofort. Sie schlagen um und zwar plötzlich. Sie kippen. Sie schlagen sogar zu. Du sitzt mir gegenüber. Ich knöpfe meine Jacke auf. Der Kellner bringt die Kerze. Er ist aus Berlin Charlottenburg. Du siehst das blaue Mieder. Kornblumenblau. Ich habe es schon mal jemand zeigen wollen. Ich habe gewartet, dass er sagt: Zieh es an. Ich habe es an. Ich zeige meine Brust, leicht, kurz, wie Rotkehlchen, das bald geschlagen wird, so knöpf ich meine Jacke auf, du sagst: Ich liebe dich. Du ziehst deinen Pullover hoch und zeigst dein Hemd. Die Brust. Lange, länger als ich mein Mieder. Dieser Moment, so hab ich mir das Leben gewünscht. Schnell, zärtlich, erkennend, schön und vorsichtig mutig, die freigesetzte Macht gebrauchen. Dann sagst du: Es nützt uns nichts. Ich sage zu schnell: Es ist trotzdem schön, du nimmst meine Hand, du sagst, dass deine Liebe zu klein ist und dass du nicht mein Mann sein willst und mich nicht

me too much, you are already flowing. You can't use me. I make the flow even stronger. I'm crying inside, because flowing is golden. You don't want me, because we are gold and we are fleeting. What crazy luxury. But you are silver too, I say, inside, when you gleam. I am ashamed that someone who has me doesn't want to have me. Who had me with just a breath. That after he said such things he took me to him, didn't speak with me, took me to him, without language, and then he spoke and said I should belong to him, more and more, and I belong to him, for the last time he thinks, more and more and he says all kinds of things like that, that I can't forget. Who am I, that it is no kind of loss to lose me? Who am I, that you think you're winning when you lose me? Don't I exist?

When two parts of shame stick into each other and fit, disquiet commences. Disquiet is not happiness. Happiness is a bomb. I like having a fever because my body burns. I find this burning not a personal thing. Whatever can get burned, I find this quite impersonal, it burns. I don't think it's a good idea to provide people with holes, it would be good enough if we could slit them.

Distance from feelings is shame. Lacking distance makes even more shame. Shame distance is a law between people, so that they don't gobble each other up, for reasons of space. It is a scandal to be as vulnerable as humans are.

Scarcely has the knife come out of the scabbard when the

haben willst, als deine Frau, die du hast, von Anfang an hattest, du willst nicht mit mir leben. Wegen dem Fliessen. Du fliesst mit mir zu sehr und fliesst schon von alleine. Du kannst mich nicht gebrauchen. Ich verstärke das Fliessen. Ich schreie innen, weil das Fliessen Gold ist. Du willst nicht, weil wir Gold sind und fliessen. Was für irrer Luxus. Du bist doch auch silbern, sag ich, innen, wenn du glänzt. Ich schäme mich, dass mich jemand, der mich hat, nicht haben will. Der mich mit einem Atemzug hatte. Dass er mich, nachdem er solche Dinge sagte, zu sich nimmt, nicht mit mir redet, zu sich nimmt, ohne Sprache, und dann redet und sagt, ich soll ihm gehören, immer mehr, und ich gehöre ihm, zum letzten Mal, denkt er, immer mehr, und er sagt viele solche Sachen, die ich nicht vergesse. Wer bin ich, dass es kein Verlust ist, mich zu verlieren? Wer bin ich, dass du gewinnst, wenn du mich verlierst, bin ich nicht da?

Wenn sich zwei Schamteile ineinanderstecken und passen, beginnt Unruhe. Unruhe ist nicht Glück. Glück ist eine Bombe. Ich habe gerne Fieber weil der Körper brennt. Ich finde dieses Brennen nicht persönlich. Was verbrannt wird, finde ich erst recht nicht persönlich, es brennt. Ich finde es keine gute Idee, Menschen mit Löchern zu versehen, es reicht doch, wenn man sie aufschneiden kann.

Abstand zum Gefühl ist Scham. Fehlender Abstand ist noch viel mehr Scham. Schamabstand ist ein Gebot zwischen Menschen, damit sie sich nicht fressen, aus Platzgründen. Es ist ein Skandal, so verletzbar zu sein wie ein Mensch.

head is rolling over the pavement and staring up at its behind. // *When the master pirate Stoertebeker is executed in Hamburg in 1402, the executioner Rosenfeld chops his head from his body. The body stands up nonetheless and staggers along the line of his pirate crew waiting their turn to be killed. The body has work to do without the head. The body always has work to do. He or it tries to save them. But Rosenfeld gets paid by the head and doesn't want to lose a victim, so he has to stop Stoertebeker's body. You can never tell what a body will do without the head. The pirate king manages to reach his eleventh man before the executioner finally throws the chopping block in front of the body's legs, so he stumbles and falls down. A body is like the rest of us and wants to save its own. But he can't save them. It is a cold day in Hamburg, they all die. They all lose their heads. And all the while his head stares up from the ground.* // Do you have to be beheaded in order not to be ashamed of your body? Have to sacrifice yourself so someone else can save his life? Nevertheless, they were all beheaded.

I'm ashamed that I'm not Matthew Barney and didn't jump tied-up into the Danube, in Budapest, that I didn't risk my life and run like a satyr deep under the water and up above have a plaintiff who sued me before the court because my sentences disturbed his intercultural marriage. I am ashamed that I am not Louise Bourgeois with adolescent boys to serve her, with vases, that I throw at photographers, and Chinese cups.

Kaum ist das Messer aus der Scheide gezogen, rollt schon der Kopf über die Strasse und glotzt zu seinem Rumpf. Störtebeker hat mit seinem abgeschnittenen Körper die Kumpane gerettet, die er abschritt, während sein Kopf vom Boden aus zusah, als Scharfrichter Rosenfeld ihm, dem Enthaupteten, beim 11. Kumpan angelangt, den Richtblock vor die Beine schmiss, weil er pro Kopf bezahlt wurde. Muss man geköpft sein, um sich nicht seines Leibes zu schämen? Muss man ihn opfern, damit ein anderer sein Leben gewinnt? Sie wurden trotzdem alle geköpft.

Ich schäme mich, dass ich nicht Matthew Barney bin und gefesselt in die Donau spring, in Budapest, dass ich nicht lebensgefährlich tief unten am Boden als Satyr im Wasser lief und oben aber einen Kläger habe, der meine Sätze verklagt vor Gericht, weil sie seine interkulturelle Ehe stören. Ich schäme mich, dass ich nicht Louise Bourgeois bin mit blutjungen Burschen zu Diensten, mit Vasen, die ich nach Fotografen schmeisse, und chinesischen Tassen.

Ich schäme mich, zu wollen, was ich will. Die Gesellschaft
will, dass wir wollen. Deshalb schäme ich mich, wenn ich gar
nichts will. Ich schäme mich in einem Café, wenn sie fragen,
was ich will, und ich will nichts. Später. Gestern. Nicht jetzt.
Oder bringen Sie mir etwas Luft. Ich schäme mich für was ich
bekam. Ich schäme mich für Dinge, die ich tun will. Ich
schäme mich, die Dinge, die ich meine, zu benennen. Ich
schäme mich für all die Leute, die ich nicht kenne. Dass wir
alle Liebe so sehr brauchen, schäm ich mich. Ich schäme mich
für die Liebe und was wir unter ihrer Flagge tun, die
stummen, obszönen, selbstmitleidig sentimentalen Plakate,
die wir durch die Strassen in unseren Demonstrationen
tragen, unseren Künsten, im Regen. Ich schäme mich für
Randomzeugs, Erinnerung an was in Fish Camp unter
Yosemite passierte. Ich schäme mich, dass ich die Namen der
Plätze will, dass ich sie, wie wer weiss was, in meinem Mund
herumrolle. Ich schäme mich für all die Namen, die ich weiss
und niemals berührte, die Städte, die ich laut nenne und nie
besuchte. Ich schäme mich für den Kamin in Albany, den
Aufzug in München und die Lounge in Carnegie Hall. Ich
schäme mich für bestimmte Dinge, die ich ansehen muss,
oder tun. Ich schäme mich fürs Vergraben und Fliegen.

Am meisten schäme ich mich, kein Tier zu sein. Ich schäme
mich mehr, nicht zu kriegen, was ich will, als es zu wollen. Ich
schäme mich, das Datum nicht zu wissen, und hier ist es
schon Mitternacht, der Tag, der, wie die Franzosen sagen,

I am ashamed of wanting what I want. Society wants us to want. So I am ashamed when I don't want anything. I am ashamed in a cafe when they say what do you want and I don't want anything. Later. Yesterday. Not now. Or bring me some air. I am ashamed of what I got. I am ashamed of things I want to do. I am ashamed to name the things I mean. I am ashamed of all the people I don't know. I am ashamed we all need love so much. I am ashamed of love and what we do under its banner, the mute self-pitying obscenely sentimental posters we carry in the street in our demonstrations, our arts, in rain. I am ashamed of random things, remembering what was done at Fish Camp under Yosemite. I am ashamed of wanting the names of places, of rolling them in my mouth like I don't know what. I am ashamed of all the names I know and never touched, the cities I recite I never visited. I am ashamed of the fireplace in Albany the elevator in Munich the lounge in Carnegie Hall. I am ashamed of certain things I need to witness or to do. I am ashamed of burrowing and flying.

Mostly I am ashamed of not being an animal. I am ashamed of not getting what I want even more than wanting it. I am ashamed of not knowing what the date is and here it's already midnight, the day the French say belongs to Saint Jean Baptiste. Because a maiden tried to overcome her shame, and dance naked in front of her attractive, fascinating, repellent step-father, poor John's head had to

Saint Jean Baptiste gehört. Weil ein Mädchen ihre Scham zu überwinden versuchte und nackt vor ihrem attraktiven, faszinierend abstossenden Stiefvater tanzte, musste er fallen, der Kopf vom armen John. Wir studieren den Tanz der Salome und schämen uns, wir studieren den blutigen Kopf, den sie an ihre Lippen hält, wie hören die toten Lippen des anderen wispern (und sie wird nie aufhören, ihn wispern zu hören): Du musst jedes Verlangen köpfen.

Ich schäme mich, so wenig zu wissen. Ich schäme mich, irgend etwas zu erinnern. Erinnerung ist eine Schande. Ich schäme mich, wie ich in der Theatinerkirche mit dir kämpfte. Ich schäme mich für das, was ich zu der Dame sagte, die ins Juwelierfenster blickte, am Graben, bevor eines der Geschäfte öffnete. Ich schäme mich für meine Fussnägel in Italien. Ich schäme mich, wie traurig meine Telefonbotschaften klingen, die ich in leeren Appartements zurücklasse, die ich später besuche und mithören muss, wenn im Zimmer nebenan die Leute die Beantworter checken, wie greift der Name daneben, das letzte, was eine Maschine kann, ist mir antworten. Kann ich dir antworten? Das letzte, was Gefühle können, ist fühlen. Ein Gefühl ist nur, was du im Moment fühlst. Später, hundert Prozent sicher, fühlst du anders. Ein Gefühl kann nicht fühlen. Nur wir. Wenn wir können. Doch Gefühle setzen uns schachmatt. Gefühle bewahren uns vor dem Fühlen. Sich so für Gefühle schämen wie für das Checken der Schlösser, der Türen und Fenster vorm Schlafen, sich so für Gefühle schämen wie dafür, die Namen der Leute auf der Strasse nicht zu wissen, die du jeden Tag siehst, das Mädchen an der

fall. We study the dance of Salome and are ashamed, we study the bloody head she holds up to her lips, we hear the dead lips of the other whisper (and she will never stop hearing him whisper it): You must decapitate each desire.

I am ashamed of knowing so little. I am ashamed of remembering anything. Memory is a shame. Memory is shame. I am ashamed of how I fought with you in the Theatinerkirche. I am ashamed of what I said to the woman gazing into the jeweler's window on the Graben before any of the stores were open. I am ashamed of my toenails in Italy. I am ashamed of how sad my voice sounds on the phone messages I leave in empty apartments I later visit and have to hear my own voice in the other room where people check their answering machines, what a misnomer, the last thing that a machine can do is answer me. Can I answer you? The last thing that feelings can do is feel. A feeling is just how you feel at the moment. Later, one hundred percent certain, later you'll feel otherwise. A feeling can't feel. Only we can feel. When we can. But feelings stymie us. Feelings keep us from feeling. Be ashamed of feelings the way you're ashamed of checking the locks on your doors and windows before you go to bed, be ashamed of feelings the way you're ashamed not to know the names of people you see every day in the street, the girl at the checkout, the old man at the carwash who doesn't actually do anything but smiles when your wet sleek car comes out of the washing tunnel. I'll never be as clean as my car, I think he means to tell me that, and I am ashamed. But sometimes

Checkoutkasse, der alte Mann an der Autowaschanlage, der wirklich nur eines tut: lächeln, wenn dein nasses schnittiges Auto aus dem Waschtunnel kommt. Ich werde nie so sauber wie mein Auto sein. Ich denke, das will er mir sagen, und ich schäme mich. Aber manchmal liegt Scham richtig. Manchmal weiss Scham mehr als Sicherheit weiss. Scham zeigt es. Und Scham hat ihre ganz eigenen Alternativen, «the kabbalah of chagrin». Scham hört sich an wie *shim*, Klemmstück, das versteckte Holzstück, das du benutzt, um wackelnde Möbelstücke zu unterlegen, // *dein disharmonisches Gestell aufzumöbeln* //, die desorganisierte Struktur meines Lebens. Scham hält mich aufrecht, Scham hält mich am Köcheln, Scham macht mich schreien. Scham macht ein Ziel aus mir, Scham, die zweitausend Jahre unterwegs war, um mich anzuklagen, alle Scham kommt zu Jedem. Von Anfang an Scham. Nur um mich zu beschämen, ist Ajax in Kuhscheisse ausgerutscht und streckte Alison ihren Hintern aus dem Fenster, die gesamte Literatur bedeutet: jeden Leser beschämen.

Lesen ist Scham, jetzt, jetzt versteh ich es. Meine Eltern sahen mich mit einem Buch in der Hand und sagten Schäm dich, du liest! Lesen ist das Studieren anderer Leute Scham, Scham, die aus den Seiten hüpft, sich in den Leser nistet. Bis an sein Lebensende. Ich schäme mich für alles. Du bist auch so. Sag nicht nein. Der Doktor wird auf solche trivialen Ausreden nicht hören. Du schämst dich für alles. Jedes Bild stempelt dich. Jedes Wort ist eine Anklage. Jedes. Jedes.

shame is right. Sometimes shame knows more than sure does. Shame tells. And shame has its own alternatives, the kabbalah of chagrin. Shame sounds like shim, the hidden shave of wood you use to prop up unbalanced furniture, the disordered structure of my life. Shame holds me up, shame keeps me bold, shame makes me shout. Shame makes a target of me, shame that has been on its way two thousand years comes to accuse me, all shame comes to everyone. Shame from the beginning. Just to shame me, Aias slipped in cowshit and Alison stuck her bottom out the window, all of literature means to shame each reader.

Reading is shame, only now I understand. My parents looked at me with a book in my hands and said Shame on you, you're reading! Reading is the study of other people's shame. Shame leaps from the page and embeds itself in the reader. Ever after. I am ashamed of everything. And so are you. Don't deny it. The doctor will not listen to such trivial excuses. You are ashamed of everything. Every image brands you. Every word is an accusation. Every. Every.

Words are contagious. A poem never stops cutting in to you, like a sliver of glass that slides under your skin one day and never leaves, always keeps journeying into the interior. Shame is that sliver of glass.

And shame is all the things that sound like itself. Resemblance itself is a crying shame, it is a shame that any given thing should make us think not just of itself in all its

Worte sind ansteckend. Ein Gedicht hört nie auf, in dich hinein zu schneiden, wie ein Glassplitter, der, eines Tages unter deine Haut geschlüpft, sie nie mehr verlässt und immer in deinem Inneren herumreist. // *Auch wenn du heiratest und deine Hand aufschneiden lässt, falls ein Splitter drin sitzt, der auf dem Weg zum Herzen ist, kannst du das Scheiden so nicht entscheiden, cutting ist kein Schnitt, der von selber geschieht, es ist ein Schnitt wie Wille, wie Absicht, wie Gewalt, wie Töten, weil es sterben muss, wenn es leben will.* // Scham ist dieser Glassplitter.

Scham, das sind alle Dinge, die sich wie sich selbst anhören. Ähnlichkeit selbst ist eine schreiende Schande, eine Schande ist es, dass alles, was es gibt, uns nicht an es denken lassen soll in all seiner Verschiedenheit, sondern an etwas anderes, was so wie es selbst ist. Ähnlichkeit ist Scham, Vergleich ist Scham, Metapher ist Scham. Ein Ding, das so tut, als sei es ein anderes Ding, ist eine Schande. // *Eine Scham, Scham wie Schande, Schande wie Scham, in sich selbst beschämend ähnlich, sich selbst gegenseitig ersetzend mit roten Schandmalschamohren. Schamschamschamscham, Scham singt auch. Kommt später.* // Scham hat viel mit so tun als ob zu tun. Scham ist, erwischt zu sein. Ich bin ein Scharlatan und bringe bestimmte heilige Medizin, die nur jene heilt, jene Spezialwesen, die meinen Lügenblödsinn glauben und in ihre Herzen nehmen. Durch solche fiese Weisheit werden sie wirklich geheilt. Geheilt durch den Namen des Einen, den du liebst. // *Name gleich Schlamassel, eine Schande von Name. Shem, Shem ist Name, Shem ist Shemesh, die Sonne, Shem ist Shimshum, Samson, der*

difference, but of some other thing like it. Resemblance is shame, comparison is shame, metaphor is shame. A thing that shams being another thing is a shame. Shame has a lot to do with sham. Shame is being found out. I am an impostor carrying certain holy medicines that will cure only those special invalids who believe my lying bullshit, and take it into their hearts. And by such vile wisdom they will actually be healed. Healed by the name of the one you love. Name = shem, shame of a name. Shem. Shem, shame of a name, of being named, of bearing a sound all the days of your life that marks you, names you as one of several, not just me, being not just the only of a kind, having family, a family to be ashamed of, shame of being recognized by strangers as being a certain kind, being one thus of many, all of them, not all of everybody but all of some, shame, of not being more different. Shem. Shame of a name, having one but never the right one, being positive inside yourself that the name you're born with is not your true name, we know our name is the root and basis of our shame, and we feel shame that the other one, the true name, will never be known, the lost name, shame of having a name that is only the shadow of what the name should be, shame that the other ones who have names all around, ones known and held and lived with and pronounced, named, they also have the wrong name whether they know it or not.

Everybody has the wrong name. Everybody is lying. Everybody should be ashamed. Really you can be friends only with someone who knows his name is wrong too.

die Sonne nieder auf den Tempel bringt, Schande von Name,
Namen, Rasselbanden, wie die Ratten der Rassel hinterher, dem
Ding vor dir, vom Fänger in die Stadt geführt, Hameln, Eden. //
Benannt worden sein, alle Tage deines Lebens einen Ton mit
dir tragen, der dich markiert, der dich als einen von vielen
nennt, nicht nur mich, nicht nur ein einziger deiner Art zu
sein, Familie zu haben, eine Familie, um sich für sie zu
schämen, die Scham, von Fremden als einer von einer
bestimmte Art erkannt zu werden, als einer bloss von vielen,
von allen von ihnen, nicht von überhaupt allen, aber von
einigen, Scham, nicht unterschiedener zu sein. Schande von
Name, einen zu haben, doch nie den richtigen, sicher sein
innen, dass der Name, mit dem du geboren bist, nicht dein
wahrer Name ist, unser Name ist Wurzel und Basis unserer
Scham, das wissen wir, und wir schämen uns, dass der andere,
der wahre Name, niemals gekannt sein wird, der verlorene
Name, die Scham, einen Namen zu haben, der nur Schatten
von dem ist, was der Name sein soll, Scham, dass all die
anderen mit ihren Namen, durch die sie gekannt sind,
gehalten, ausgesprochen sind, // *in die Welt gestellt* //, auch
falsche Namen haben, ob sie es wissen oder nicht.

Jeder hat den falschen Namen. Jeder lügt. Jeder sollte sich
schämen. Weisst du, du kannst nur mit wem befreundet sein,
der weiss wie du, der eigene Name ist falsch. *Shem.* Scham,
immer falsch zu sein, falsch unter Falschen zu sein, als ob man
in Wirklichkeit wundervoll, versteckterweise ein Prinz ist in
Wahrheit, nur das falsche Land, ein anderes kleines
Bergkönigtum schmerzhaft weit weg, nicht dieses, nicht hier,

Shame of being the wrong one always, being a wrong one with wrong ones, as if one really, wonderfully, hiddenly is a prince in truth, but of the wrong country, another little mountain kingdom painfully far away, not this one, not here, never here. Shame of never being here. Shame of always having to go. Go to the bathroom and look in the mirror and there is the fountain of shame, the charlatan's face, the one you never mean. Go to the city and be nobody, go to the country and be alone with your shame. Go to the doctor. The doctor tastes your urine and gazes into your eyes. Shame of being known. One is a prince, the Prince of Shame, o Nameless the Last, Prince of Shame. But Shame is my little horse. Shame is the plain girl who took me to the dance. Shame happens hard and soft, it seethes or even soothes, because when you're shamed you can't be worse. There is a leveling in things, the plain of shame, auf der Schamenheide sich troesten treue Lieber and there we meet, amateurs of love, clumsy lovers at a traveling circus in a power failure, every place is wrong, this wrong excites us, we have to find a place to lay our shame down and comfort it. Let shame comfort us. Flooded with remorse, shame hurts less. Religions work by turning shame into remorse. Remorse becomes just history, not now. Never now. So shame, which is never-being-here, is cured by not-being-now.

niemals hier. Scham, niemals hier zu sein. Scham, immer gehen zu müssen. Geh ins Badezimmer und schau in den Spiegel, da ist die Schamfontäne, das Scharlatangesicht, der eine, den du niemals meinst. Geh in die Stadt und sei niemand, geh aufs Land und sei allein mit deiner Scham. Geh zum Doktor. Der Doktor probiert deinen Urin und blickt in deine Augen. Scham, gekannt zu sein. Einer ist ein Prinz, der Prinz der Scham, o Schamfürst Namenlos der Letzte. Aber Scham ist mein kleines Pferd. Scham ist das unansehnliche Mädchen, das mich zum Tanz nimmt. Scham passiert hart und weich, schäumt oder beschwichtigt sogar, wer sich schämt, dem kann es nicht schlimmer gehen. Es gibt einen Ausgleich unter den Dingen, der Ebene der Scham, *auf der Schamenheide sich trösten treue Lieber* und da treffen wir uns, Amateure der Liebe, unbeholfene Liebende eines fahrenden Zirkus mitten beim Stromausfall, jeder Platz ist falsch, dieses Falsch regt uns auf, wir müssen einen Platz finden, um unsere Scham niederzulegen und sie zu trösten. Soll Scham uns trösten. Überströmt mit Bedauern, verletzt sie, die Scham, weniger. Religionen funktionieren, indem sie die Scham umdrehen, ins Bedauern. Bedauern wird sofort Geschichte, nicht jetzt. Niemals jetzt. So wird die Scham, niemals hier zu sein, geheilt durch jetzt nicht hier sein.

Shame 5

But shame is my little horse. I like this sentence. It's like a pony. If I were lighter, it could carry me. I am ashamed of my weight. I am ashamed that I've never been lifted up,

SCHAM 5

But shame is my little horse. Ich mag diesen Satz. Er ist wie ein Pony. Wenn ich leichter wäre, trüge es mich. Ich schäme mich für mein Gewicht. Ich schäme mich, nie aufgehoben, nie

never safely, never been swung about, never been able to be carried. I am a colossus. I saw this horse on television. The horse psychiatrist sat down every day in the pasture and stroked its saddle until the sun went down. (Sun stands for shamelessness.) The saddle lay across his knees. (Knees stand for humility.) One day the horse came up from behind and nudged the horse psychiatrist. The horse psychiatrist gave no hint of his pleasure and went on stroking the saddle till the sun went down. After four weeks the horse came up and sniffed at his shirt. The horse came from far away. It was undergoing a treatment. It was something with a little girl on its back, a truck in front of its startled hooves, and fire was part of it, and a second girl who's dead. She was dragged on the ground by a second horse. The second horse is also dead and was in despair before that. In parallel with the healing of the horse and of the limping girl, the horse psychiatrist was concerned with the mother, who was in a marital crisis and at a dangerous standstill of her instincts. The horse psychiatrist had the girl drive the Range Rover for the first time and had the mother ride horses bareback in the desert. Mother and daughter change again, the horse keeps coming closer. Feelings pass between the people. One time the mother and the horse psychiatrist dance and hold each other back. The husband and father appears. The time set for the return journey is the healing. The decision depends on the horse, and it fails. It remembers. Everybody is watching from outside the fence. Only the girl is inside, standing next to the horse, one unit of trauma. If the horse psychiatrist doesn't succeed, the

in Sicherheit, nie geschaukelt, nie getragen gewesen zu sein. Ich bin ein Koloss. Ich sah dieses Pferd im Fernsehen. Der Pferdepsychiater setzte sich jeden Tag in die Koppel und strich seinen Sattel, bis die Sonne unterging. (Sonne steht für Schamlosigkeit.) Der Sattel lag auf seinen Knien. (Knie steht für Demut.) Eines Tages kam das Pferd von hinten und stupste den Pferdepsychiater. Der Pferdepsychiater verlieh seiner Freude keinen Ausdruck und strich seinen Sattel, bis die Sonne unterging. Nach vier Wochen schnupperte das Pferd an seinem Hemd. Das Pferd kommt von weit her. Es macht eine Kur. Es ist etwas mit einem kleinen Mädchen auf seinem Rücken, einem Lastwagen vor seinen hochgeschreckten Hufen, und Feuer passiert, und einem zweiten Mädchen, das tot ist. Es wurde von einem zweiten Pferd am Boden geschleift. Das zweite Pferd ist ebenfalls tot und war vorher verzweifelt. Parallel zur Heilung des Pferdes und des humpelnden Mädchens ist der Pferdepsychiater mit der Mutter beschäftigt, die in einer Ehekrise steckt und in einem gefährlichen Stillstand ihrer Instinkte. Der Pferdepsychiater lässt das Mädchen zum ersten Mal Range Rover fahren und die Mutter sattellose Pferde in der Wildnis reiten. Mutter und Tochter bewegen sich wieder, das Pferd kommt immer näher. Zwischen den Menschen passieren Gefühle. Einmal tanzen Mutter und Pferdepsychiater und zügeln sich. Der Mann und Vater erscheint. Der Zeitpunkt für die Rückreise ist die Heilung. Das Pferd trägt die Entscheidung, und es versagt. Es erinnert sich. Alle hinter dem Gatter sehen zu, nur das Mädchen steht innen beim Pferd, eine Traumaeinheit. Wenn der Pferdepsychiater nicht

family is a tragedy. The horse psychiatrist twitches the lasso and is going to use force. The front hooves are bound and the horse is compelled by whipping to run in a circle. It collapses, stands up again, is thrashed, collapses, till it just lies there. When I was 16, they said surrender was like that. The word is: a sacrifice. So the horse is lying there broken. // *Tamed.* // Its eyes come out of trauma, says the camera. They shove the curtain back. The veil on the eyes of the horse is gone. Technically that was done with eye drops. Really it's karma as camera. The girl strokes the trembling horse and climbs on. The mother, without consulting the daughter, gives the horse to the horse psychiatrist, and returns alone.

You're ashamed of everything, ashamed of yourself above all, especially in front of the horse. You would have liked to experience with bound hooves all over again the horse and the compulsion, the truck, the fire and the dead girl. You would have liked to be bound and sink out of breath to the ground, to bear it your whole life long. Trust. You would have liked wiping the film out of your eyes. The whole recollection turns back. Magic of the violent action. The resurrection program. Love for the horse psychiatrist. Obey somebody blindly. Yield yourself completely. Fetch bananas for the Master, and so on. To be incorporated into a necessarily immanent will, of your own free will being bound, possessed.

You're ashamed of the girl who sees this, she strokes the

siegt, ist die Familie eine Tragödie. Der Pferdepsychiater zückt das Lasso und wird Gewalt gebrauchen. Die vorderen Hufe werden gebunden, und das Pferd wird mit der Peitsche gezwungen, im Kreis zu laufen. Es knickt ein, steht wieder auf, wird gedroschen, knickt ein, bis es liegen bleibt. Als ich 16 war, sagten sie surrender zu so was. Das Wort ist: Opfer. Dann liegt das Pferd gebrochen da. Seine Augen kommen zurück aus dem Trauma, sagt die Kamera. Sie schieben den Vorhang zurück. Der Schleier auf dem Auge des Pferdes ist weg. Technisch war das mit Augentropfen zu machen. Real ist es Karma als Kamera. Das Mädchen streichelt das zitternde Pferd und steigt auf. Die Mutter schenkt dem Pferdepsychiater, ohne die Tochter zu fragen, das Pferd und kehrt selbst zurück.

Du schämst dich für alle, vor allem für dich, besonders vorm Pferd. Du wärst gerne das Pferd und gezwungen, den Lastwagen, das Feuer und das tote Mädchen wieder zu erleben mit gebundenen Hufen. Du wärst gerne gefesselt und ausser Atem zu Boden gegangen, um es dann dein Leben lang zu tragen. Vertrauen. Du hättest gerne den Film aus deinen Augen gewischt. Das ganze Gedächtnis zurückgedreht. Die Magie der harten Tour. Das Auferstehungsprogramm. Die Liebe zum Pferdepsychiater. Jemandem blind gehorchen. Sich übergeben. Dem Meister Bananen bringen, etc. Einem notwendigen immanenten Willen einverleibt sein, freiwillig gebunden, zugehörig.

Du schämst dich für das Mädchen, das zusieht, es streichelt

horse and mounts it, ashamed of how she trusts Clint
Eastwood. It's not Clint Eastwood. You sink into the ground
when you see anyone who has trust in anyone. Or devotion,
you're ashamed of the word. And how she's jealous of her
mother and Clint Eastwood. You're ashamed of the horse
that joins in the play. You're ashamed of the sofa. You'd like
to see a movie where a horse sits on a man. Pipi
Longstockings lifts the pale horse into the air. When it
comes to animals, people have stupid ideas, even the good
ones. Nietzsche broke down and cried in the street and
leaned his head against the cheek of the whipped horse, that
was his last action in freedom. Pipi Longstockings is an all-
powerful girl with two I's in her name. I's are sharp, haughty
as towers and they want to frighten God. You pronounce
your name guilty because of your appearance. You can't
imagine being guilty about that. You weren't even there yet,
and had a name of your own already. You live in the verdict.
Your father doesn't want you to get more schooling than he
did, if you're a girl. Your father at sixteen was in a U-boat.
You're ashamed that you're not dead, and you save things
up. You hoard proverbs, sentences, feelings, pictures, books,
names, furniture, snapshots, reminiscences, discoveries,
shoes, clothes, food, money, love letters, pain, etc. You let
nothing go. You are a colossus. Nobody can hold you.
Except the one who says that he can hold you, on the
heights of Fulda in the train in the compartment, that lies in
deep sleep for you, I can hold you, that isn't a promise, it is
what he can do and doesn't want to do, since that would
make him nobody, oh, he says, if you caress him, there'll be

und aufsitzt, und wie es Clint Eastwood vertraut. Es war nicht Clint Eastwood. Du sinkst in den Boden, wenn du jemanden siehst, der jemandem vertraut. Oder Hingabe, du schämst dich für das Wort. Und wie es eifersüchtig auf seine Mutter ist und Clint Eastwood. Du schämst dich für das Pferd, das mitspielt. Du schämst dich für das Sofa. Du möchtest einen Film sehen, auf dem ein Pferd auf einem Menschen sitzt. Pipi Langstrumpf stemmt den Schimmel in die Luft. Was Tiere betrifft haben Menschen blöde Gedanken, selbst gute. Nietzsche hat auf der Strasse geweint und seinen Kopf an die Wange des geschundenen Pferdes gelehnt, das war seine letzte Handlung in Freiheit. Pippi Langstrumpf ist ein Mädchen der Allmacht mit zwei i's im Namen. I's sind spitz, hochmütig wie Türme und wollen Gott erschrecken. Du sprichst deinen Namen schuldig für dein Aussehen. Du kannst dir nicht vorstellen, selbst daran schuld zu sein. Du warst noch nicht da und hattest schon einen Namen. Du lebst im Urteil. Dein Vater will nicht, dass du mehr Schule kriegst als er, wenn du ein Mädchen bist. Dein Vater war mit 16 im U-Boot. Du schämst dich, dass du nicht tot bist, und hortest. Du hortest Worte, Sätze, Gefühle, Bilder, Bücher, Namen, Möbel, Fotos, Erinnerungen, Erfindungen, Schuhe, Kleider, Essen, Geld, Liebesbriefe, Schmerz, etc. Nichts lässt du los. Du bist ein Koloss. Niemand kann dich halten. Ausser jemand, der sagt, dass er dich halten kann, auf der Höhe von Fulda im Zug im Abteil, das für euch im Tiefschlaf liegt, ich kann dich halten, das ist kein Versprechen, es ist das, was er kann und nicht will, weil er dabei niemand wird, o, sagt er, wenn du ihn streichelst, mich gibt es gleich nicht mehr, ich bin niemand. Du liebst

no me any more, I am nobody. You love Nobody. You would
even love to be nobody yourself, when he caresses you.

SCHAM 6

Scham ist ein weisser Baum. *Ich bin war.* Jetzt ist damals. Ich
war falsch, nicht ein Pferd. Scham ist ein weisser Baum. Ich
weiss es wenn. *I am was.* // *Das Pferd ist nicht zuhaus, horse,
mein englisches Pferd, ist dein deutsches Haus.* // Vergangen ist
nicht vergangen. Das stimmt, das ist wirklich Scham, die
Vergangenheit vergeht nicht, die Toten riechen nicht tot.
Schimmelige, verwelkte Blätter, ihr Geruch im Wind, im
Herbst, doch bringt das Licht der Sonne etwas mit. Von
überall kommt es her, um hier zu sein. Hier ist so ein
schmales Messer, es geht hier, das ist der Punkt, um alles. Hier
heisst die Geschichte, die ich nicht erzählen will. Nicht
Copperhead, Kupferkopf, die Giftschlange, die wir gerade
gesehen haben, klein, unter einen gefallenen Zweig geringelt.
Copperhead, eine Giftschlange, die mich einmal gebissen hat.
Aber das ist eine andere Geschichte. Die Geschichte heisst
Furcht, nicht Scham. Nicht die, die mich vor fünfzig Jahren
biss. Das jedoch ist eine Geschichte mit nichts Schlimmem
drin ausser ich. Keine Schlange nötig. Das ist, was Scham ist,
eine Geschichte, die nur mich in sich hat.

Allein sein und falsch sein, das ist Scham. Das Gegenteil von
Scham ist nicht Ruhm, das Gegenteil ist Heiligkeit, allein sein
und richtig sein. Doch was ist falsch. Falsch ist, etwas tun, was
nicht vergeht, jedes anständige Ding weiss, dass es fort muss.

Niemand. Du würdest es lieben, selber, niemand zu sein, wenn er dich streichelt.

SHAME 6

Shame is a white tree. Ich bin war. Now is then. I was wrong, not a horse. Shame is a white tree. I know it when. I am was. The past is not the past. This is true, this is what shame really is, the past that does not pass, the dead who don't smell dead. Smell of leaf mold on an autumn wind, for all the sunlight something's carrying. From everywhere it comes to be here. Here is such a narrow knife, the point of everywhere. Here means the story I don't want to tell. Not the copperhead we just saw, small, looped below a fallen twig. Copperhead, a venomous serpent that bit me once. But that's another story. The story called fear, not the story called shame. Not the one that bit me fifty years ago. This however is a story with nothing bad in it but me. No snake needed. That is what shame is, a story that has only me in it.

Shame is being alone and being wrong. The opposite of shame is not glory, the opposite is sanctity, which is being alone and being right. But what is wrong. Wrong is doing something that does not pass away, any decent thing knows enough to be gone. Wrong is staying too long. In the Bible the Lord was ashamed of humans and what they did, what they do, so he called a great Flood to wipe them out, men and their works. But humans were the work and deed of the Lord, so the Lord was ashamed of what he had done,

Falsch ist, zu lang bleiben. In der Bibel schämte sich der Herr
für die Menschen und was sie taten, was sie tun, deshalb hiess
er die grosse Flut, sie hinaus zu fegen, die Menschen und ihre
Arbeiten. Die Menschen aber waren die Arbeit und Tat des
Herrn, so schämte sich der Herr für das, was er getan hatte,
den Menschen nach seinem Bild formen, seinem Mass,
mashal. Scham ist mashal, Gleichnis, Ähnlichkeit, Parabel. Die
Geschichte der Flut ist die Geschichte des Herausfegens der
Vergangenheit. Das ist es. Es klappte nicht. Es gibt Menschen
und Regen und Trockenheit und der breite Yamuna kriecht
durch die zwanzig Millionen Leute in New Delhi, seicht und
schimmernd im Abendlicht, hüpfende Moskitos, und nichts
ging jemals verloren. Die Flut tötete, doch löschte nicht.
Vielleicht kann sie es nie. Was ist, ist. Es bleibt. Aus der
Flutebene schreien wir auf, Gott, lass, was ist, wieder gehen.
Doch nichts geht. Die Scham bleibt. Der Falke überm
Swimmingpool, was sieht er, was braucht er. Eine winzige
Wolkenverschiebung, sonst nichts. Erst als ich es studiere,
verdichtet es sich, wird flüssig. Der Falke ist weg. Dann ist er
wieder da. Wie Scham. Scham ist ein Vogel, der den Himmel
reitet, der Himmel ist etwas, was nie weg geht. Stell dir vor:
kein Himmel. Kein Raum. Schon wenn du beginnst, zu
versuchen, dir keinen Raum vorzustellen, musst du dir Raum
vorstellen für kein Raum, von dem du ausgeschlossen oder in
den du eingeschlossen bist. Kontraktion, Tzimtzum des Ari //
das Wort Rabbis Isaak Luria, «Der Löwe» genannt – Tzimtzum
bedeutet Zurücknahme des Lichts, Einschränkung. // Schwarzes
Loch. Scham. Weil sie über Scham ist, muss sie über mich
sein, diese Geschichte. Die Kontraktion von jemand bis zu

making man according to his image and his mashal, his simile or likeness. The story of the Flood is the story of wiping out the past. And here we are. It did not succeed. Men exist, and rain, and drought, and the broad Yamuna creeps through the twenty million people of New Delhi shallow shimmering with evening light, skittering with mosquitoes and nothing has ever been lost. The Flood killed but did not erase. Maybe it never can. What is, is. It stays. We cry out from the flood plain, God, let a thing be gone. But nothing goes. Shame stays. Hawk over swimming pool, what does he see, what does he need. One tiny blur of cloud and nothing else. Only as I study it, it condenses. The hawk is gone. Then it's back again. Like shame. Shame is a bird that rides on the sky, the sky is a thing that never goes away. Imagine no sky. No space. Even to begin to try to imagine no space, you have to imagine a space for no space to be in or be excluded from. Contraction, tzimtzum of the Ari. Black Hole. Shame. The story, since it is about shame, has to be about me. The contraction of someone to the smallest dimensions, the smallest self he is. The shame is being so little, so much less. The shame is me, is a black hole. There was an autumn night, it was always night when I was young, day wasn't known yet, the time when men wear hats and go to work, my mother said I turned night into day but really I turned day into night, it was always night. I was drunk, and with drunken friends I walked around. But this is not about friends, not at all. Whoever they were. Who can remember the names of drunken friends. I think one was French and one was a surrealist and

seiner kleinsten Dimension, das kleinste Selbst, das er ist. Die Scham ist die, so wenig zu sein, so viel weniger. Die Scham ist ich, ich ist ein schwarzes Loch. Es war eine Herbstnacht, es war immer Nacht, als ich jung war, den Tag, die Zeit, wenn Männer Hüte tragen und zur Arbeit gehen, gab es noch nicht, meine Mutter sagte, ich mache die Nacht zum Tag, in Wirklichkeit machte ich den Tag zur Nacht, es war immer Nacht. Ich war betrunken und zog mit betrunkenen Freunden rum. Doch das hier ist nicht über Freunde, überhaupt nicht. Wer auch immer sie waren. Wer kann sich an die Namen betrunkener Freunde erinnern. Ich glaube, einer war Franzose und einer Surrealist und einer war immer betrunken, während wir nur ab und zu betrunken waren, ein oder zweimal die Woche vielleicht, je nachdem, womit uns die Flasche beglückte. Das Orakel wurde durch die Strassen getragen. Bernsteinorakel. Doch hier geht es nicht um das Orakel, das Orakel ist immer falsch. Es geht nicht um uns, nur um mich, wir kamen in einen Hof im Westen der Stadt, einer dieser gepflasterten Plätze zwischen den Häusern an der Strasse und dem Hinterhaus, wo die älteren Häuser stehen, heimlich, du würdest sie niemals von der Strasse aus vermuten. Scham ist, was du niemals von der Strasse aus vermutest. Ein Betrunkener denkt, er sei unsichtbar. Selbst wenn er singt. Der Falke denkt, er sei im Himmel unsichtbar. Jeden Moment lang wartet das Wasser.

Scham wartet immer. Das hört sich nicht nach sehr viel an. Was hast du getan? Ich habe einen Baum verletzt.

one was someone who was drunk all the time whereas we were drunk just once in a while, once or twice a week maybe, as the luck of the bottle allowed. The oracle we carried around through the streets. Amber oracle. But it's not about the oracle, the oracle is always wrong. It's not about us, just me, we had turned into a courtyard in the West Village, one of those cobbled areas between the house on the street and the house out back, where the older houses stood, secret, you'd never guess it from the street. Shame is what you'd never guess from the street. A drunken man thinks he is invisible. Even if he sings. A hawk thinks he is invisible in the sky. Moment by moment the water waits.

Shame is always waiting. It doesn't sound like much. What did you do? I hurt a tree.

There was some purpose that led us down the dark hallway through the front building to the courtyard, I still feel the cobblestones under my old shoes but I can't remember the purpose. We were drunk and there was supposed to be a party in the rear building. Always going back, like pederasts or etymologists, the sacred road runs backwards into the interior, via sacra, pia sacra, pia puella introita, how did we think I don't know, how I was thinking was how I am always thinking, find, find her, where is she. If a shadow passes over the page, over the pool, over the mountainside down the maples and hemlocks, it is she, not a hawk not a cloud but the one I must be after, the one every drunken man is after,

Es gab da einen Grund, der uns durch den dunklen Gang durch das Vordergebäude in den Hof gehen liess, ich fühle immer noch die Pflastersteine unter meinen alten Schuhen, doch den Grund erinnere ich nicht. Wir waren betrunken und im Hintergebäude sollte eine Party sein. Die Strasse geht immerzu zurück, wie Päderasten oder Etymologen, via sacra, heiliger Weg, pia mater, Gehirnmutter, pia puella introita, holde Jungfrau, eingedrungene, wie wir darauf kamen, weiss ich nicht, ich dachte, was ich immer dachte, finde, finde sie, wo ist sie. Wenn ein Schatten über die Seiten streift, über den Pool, über die Bergseite, Ahorn und Schierling, ist sie es, kein Falke, keine Wolke, doch diese Eine, hinter der ich her sein muss, die Eine, hinter der jeder Betrunkene her ist, trinken, um sie zu finden, und zu betrunken, um sie zu finden, betrunken, weil er sie nicht finden kann, kann er sie nicht finden, weil er zu betrunken ist, doch wäre er nicht betrunken, würde er sich nicht nach ihr umsehen, sie suchen, hier, sich nach ihr in Hinterhäusern umsehen. Scham ist ein Hinterhaus. Die ganze Zeit zurücksehen. Scham ist zurücksehen, gezwungen dazu, kann nicht aufhören. Eines Morgens wachte ich in Leipzig auf. Beim vorzüglichen und reichhaltigen Frühstück im Hotel Maritim, ein sozialistischer Meilenstein, plante ich meinen Tag. Ich war noch nie vorher in Sachsen gewesen. Ich wollte die Thomaskirche besuchen, wo Bach lebte und spielte. Der Hotelier gab mir eine Wegbeschreibung und den Stadtplan, mein Weg führte über den Sachsenplatz. Als ich den Plan las, erinnerte ich mich plötzlich an eine Nacht vor vielen Jahrzehnten. Ich war betrunken und fuhr in einer Untergrundbahn in Queens, eine

drink to find her and too drunk to find her, drunk because
he can't find her and can't find her because he's drunk, but
if he weren't drunk he wouldn't let himself be looking, be
looking for her, here, looking for her in rear buildings.
Shame is a rear building. Looking backwards all the time.
Shame is looking backwards, compelled to, can't stop. One
morning I woke up in Leipzig. Over the excellent and ample
breakfast at the Hotel Maritim, a socialist landmark, I was
planning my day. I had never been in Saxony before. I
wanted to visit the Thomaskirche, where Bach lived and
played. The hotelier gave me directions and a plan of the
city, my route marked down the Sachsenplatz. As I read the
map, I suddenly remembered a night many decades before.
I was drunk and riding on the subway in Queens, but on a
line that came out and ran above the ground, in daylight,
drunk in daylight. I was with some people. Later, when I
was sober, one of them told me that I had, with drunken
persistence, insisted on speaking German. He was German.
He said I spoke surprisingly well, and that I actually spoke
with a Saxon accent, and sounded like someone from
Leipzig, a drunken young man from Leipzig. But now I'm
not sure if I thought of that in Leipzig, that morning,
leaving the Maritim, or if I'm only remembering it now,
and observing two isolated and separated instances of
Leipzig. Later that night, the Leipzig not the Queens night, I
found myself on a stage giving a reading from my work, and
found it required me to ad lib in German. I'm not sure if I
remembered it then. The shame of not remembering the
shame of being drunk inside the shame of speaking a

Linie, die über der Erde fuhr, im Tageslicht, betrunken im Tageslicht. Ich war mit einigen Leuten zusammen. Später, als ich nüchtern war, erzählte mir einer von ihnen, ich hätte mit betrunkener Hartnäckigkeit darauf bestanden, Deutsch zu sprechen. Er war Deutscher. Er sagte, ich habe überraschend gut gesprochen, und dass ich tatsächlich mit einem sächsischen Akzent gesprochen hätte, wie jemand aus Leipzig, ein betrunkener junger Mann aus Leipzig. Doch jetzt bin ich nicht sicher, ob ich in Leipzig daran dachte, an jenem Morgen, als ich das Maritim verliess, oder ob ich es nur jetzt und zwei isolierte und getrennte Leipziger Momente erinnere. Später in dieser Nacht, der Leipzignacht, nicht der Queensnacht, fand ich mich auf einer Bühne wieder, ich las aus meinem Werk, und fand es nötig, aus dem Stegreif eine deutsche Lippe zu riskieren. Ich bin nicht sicher, ob ich es damals erinnerte. Die Scham, sich nicht an die Scham zu erinnern, betrunken zu sein, im Inneren der Scham, eine Sprache zu sprechen, die ich nicht kann. Die Scham, in Leipzig auf einer Bühne zu stehen und mich an ein gebildetes, schwarz gekleidetes und rauchendes Publikum zu wenden, das zu mir hochsah, als ich in seiner Sprache redete, hilfreich und freundlich, so wie Menschen einem Hund bei einem schwierigen Kunststück mit einem Stöckchen zusehen und die Daumen drücken. Scham hat immer ein neues Gesicht, die Scham, ihre Sprache nicht richtig zu sprechen, was sag ich zu ihnen, was teile ich mit ihnen, die Scham, zu reden, die Scham, nicht mal zu rauchen, die Scham, nicht mal betrunken zu sein. Die Scham der Sprache. Die Scham der Sprache. // *Der Charme der Sprache liegt im Wiederholen wie ein Beinchen begraben.* //

language I don't know. The shame of standing on a platform in Leipzig addressing a sophisticated audience dressed in black and smoking cigarettes, they looked up at me speaking in their language, they looked up helpfully and kindly, the way men watch a difficult trick being performed by a dog and a stick, hoping for the best. Shame always has a new face, the shame of not speaking someone else's language really, what am I saying to them, what am I sharing, the shame of saying, the shame of not even smoking, the shame of not even being drunk. The shame of language. The shame of language.

What does it mean? Sounding like Leipzig then being in Leipzig and not remembering, I'm sure now I didn't remember then, I'm sure it was just today and today and try to speak German, try to make them understand why I was standing there, the shame of standing there with nothing but my words to tell them, my words which were in English embedded in the other language, theirs, that I distorted to tell them, shame of having to tell them, here I am. What does it mean? What do things mean? It seems such a shame if such things mean nothing. It should mean something that a drunken schoolboy speaks Leipzig German. It should mean something that this same boy decades later finds himself in Leipzig able more or less to communicate his desires and discuss their satisfaction, he has this map in his hand, it must mean something, he walks by the blue and yellow Saxon state flowers, down past the Stasi headquarters and the pretty women waiting for the bus,

Was heisst das? Hört sich nach Leipzig an, in Leipzig sein und sich nicht erinnern daran, nun bin ich sicher, ich hab mich da nicht erinnert daran, ich bin sicher, es war nur heute und heute und der Versuch, Deutsch zu sprechen, der Versuch, ihnen zu sagen, warum ich da stehe, die Scham, da zu stehen mit nichts als meinen Worten, meine Worte, die im Englischen eingelassen waren in die andere Sprache, ihre, die ich entstellte, um es ihnen sagen zu können, die Scham, ihnen sagen zu müssen, hier bin ich. Was heisst das? Was bedeuten die Dinge? Es scheint eine solche Schande zu sein, wenn solche Sachen nichts bedeuten. Es sollte etwas bedeuten, dass ein betrunkener Schuljunge Leipzigdeutsch spricht. Es sollte etwas bedeuten, dass sich dieser Junge Jahrzehnte später in Leipzig wiederfindet, wie er mehr oder weniger seine Wünsche kommunizieren kann und ihre Befriedigung diskutieren, er hat diesen Plan in seiner Hand, es muss etwas bedeuten, er geht die blauen und gelben Sachsenstaatblumen entlang, am Stasihauptquartier vorbei, und die hübschen Frauen warten auf den Bus, zum Museum runter, wo er die Gesichter derselben Frauen auf alten Leinwänden in leeren warmen Räumen sieht. Es muss etwas bedeuten. Es bedeutet, dass er versucht, nicht die andere Geschichte zu erzählen, die betrunkene über den Baum, über mich.

Er steht nun, nein, das ist nicht Sachsen, diese Geschichte ist Scham, so steh ich nun betrunken in einem gepflasterten Hof in der Bedford Street mit meinen betrunkenen Freunden. Einer der Freunde ist ins Hinterhaus gegangen zur Party, von der wir hörten, durch die Gerüchte über Trinken und Frauen

down to the museum where he sees the faces of the same women on old canvases in empty warm rooms. It must mean something. It means that he is trying not to tell the other story, the drunken one about the tree, about me.

He is standing, no, this is not Saxony, this story is shame, so I am standing drunk in a cobbled courtyard off Bedford Street with my drunken friends. One of the friends has gone into the rear building to find the party we have heard about, drawn by the rumor of drink and women. There is a problem. I do not remember the problem. He didn't come out. There was no party. There was a party but we were denied access. The party was boring and unappealing. The wrong people. The wrong night. He didn't come out. He was in there making out with some woman. He was having a fight with some man. He had lost his motivation, drunks do, he had wandered off into the night through some other exit. There we stood, waiting, and nothing was happening. It seems there was no party. No anything. All there was was what I felt. That is what shame is. Shame is when there is nothing but what you feel. Feeling is shame. I am ashamed of feelings when there is nothing there but feeling.

What I felt was the vast pressure of the obstacle. The stone of the world crushing my door closed. Something huge and potent and abstract, as if in that quiet cobbled yard we stood close to the Denying Force itself. Ich bin der Geist der stets verneint would have come into my head then, I knew all the famous lines, what good did it do me, what I knew or

angezogen. Da ist ein Problem. Ich erinnere mich nicht an das Problem. Er kam nicht raus. Da war keine Party. Da war eine Party, doch uns war der Zugang verwehrt. Die Party war langweilig und reizlos. Die falschen Leute. Die falsche Nacht. Er kam nicht raus. Er war drinnen und trieb es mit irgendeiner Frau. Er hatte einen Kampf mit irgendeinem Typen. Er hatte seine Motivation verloren, das passiert Betrunkenen, er hatte sich durch einen anderen Ausgang in die Nacht davongemacht. Da standen wir, wartend, nichts passierte. Es schien, da war keine Party. Kein Irgendwas. Alles, was da war, war, was ich fühlte. Das ist, was Scham ist. Scham ist, wenn nichts ist, ausser was du fühlst. Fühlen ist Scham. Ich schäme mich für die Gefühle, wenn nichts anderes da ist als Fühlen.

Was ich fühlte, war der grosse Druck des Gegenstands. Der Stein der Welt schmiss meine Tür zu. Etwas Riesiges, Potentes und Abstraktes, als ob wir in diesem ruhigen gepflasterten Hof ganz nah vor der Verneinenden Macht selber stünden. *Ich bin der Geist, der stets verneint* wäre mir dann in meinen Kopf gekommen, ich wusste all die berühmten Zeilen, und was bringt es mir, was ich wusste, oder erinnerte? Keinerlei Transmutation. Scham ist, wenn Erinnerung ist, ohne Transmutation, Scham ist Vergangenheit ohne Gegenwart. Ich war betrunken und allein und bitter und wild, weit weg vom Schloss der Jungfern und dem ummauerten Garten der Liebe, dies war ein anderer Hof, ein Mann versiegelt in sein Schicksal, ein weisser Baum, ein Verhängnis, eine Banalität, ein Tod. Ich war allein auf den Pflastersteinen, allein auf die

remembered. There is no transmutation. Shame is when there is memory without transmutation, shame is a past without a present. I was drunk and alone and bitter and fierce, far from the Castle of Maidens and the walled garden of Love, this was another courtyard, a man sealed in with his fate, a white tree, a doom, a banality, a death. I was alone on the cobblestones, alone in the worst way. The worst way to be alone is to be with companions who mean nothing. They were not the ones I wanted, who could not help me in my quest, who could only hinder, drunken oafs like me, alone with one another. In an empty courtyard, an empty night we were too feeble to populate with intelligence or dance. Near to me I felt that the mean world had focused all his Denying Force, the devil power in the world that made me poor, lonely, inept, unhealthy, solitary, drunk, unhappy drunk unhappy sober, the force that negated everything I wanted, everything I could be. The force that negated me.

In the courtyard grew a tree. A white sapling, birch, a few years old. It stood out of a two foot square of dirt hemmed in by stone. I was drunk, I was unhappy, I didn't know why and didn't know anything at all worth knowing. Shame is a white tree. I wrapped my arms around this tree and groaned and heaved it out of the ground. Shame is a white tree. All my life I come back to that terrible moment and I shudder and blood rushes to my face and I feel deep shame. I killed a tree, I pulled it out of the ground, a lovely white young tree, all done with its work for winter, all that is bad enough. But how I did it, the mind that ran me as I did it, a

schlimmste Weise. Die schlimmste Weise, allein zu sein, ist mit Leuten zu sein, die einem nichts bedeuten. Sie waren nicht die, die ich wollte, sie konnten mir nicht helfen in meiner Suche, nur behindern, betrunkene Rüpel wie ich, allein miteinander. In einem leeren Hof, einer leeren Nacht, waren wir zu schwach, um uns selbst mit Intelligenz oder Tanz anzureichern. In meiner Nähe fühlte ich die gemeine Welt alle ihre verneinende Macht in den Brennpunkt rücken, die Teufelskraft in der Welt, die mich arm machte, allein, unfähig, ungesund, einsam, betrunken, unglücklich, unglücklich betrunken, unglücklich nüchtern, die Macht, die alles negierte, was ich wollte, was ich sein könnte. Die Macht, die mich verneinte.

Im Hof wuchs ein Baum. Ein weisser Schössling, Birke, ein paar Jahre alt. Sie ragte aus einem zwei Fuss grossen Quadrat aus Dreck, gehalten durch Steine. Ich war betrunken. Ich war unglücklich. Ich wusste nicht warum und wusste nichts, was zu wissen wert war. Scham ist ein weisser Baum. Ich schlang meine Arme um den Baum, stöhnte und hiefte ihn aus dem Grund. Scham ist ein weisser Baum. Mein ganzes Leben lang komme ich zurück zu diesem schrecklichen Moment und ich schauder, Blut schiesst mir ins Gesicht und ich fühle tiefe Scham. Ich tötete einen Baum, ich zog ihn aus dem Grund, einen lieblichen weissen jungen Baum, fertig mit seiner Vorbereitung für den Winter, all das ist schlimm genug. Aber wie ich es tat, der Geist, der mich befiel, als ich es tat, ein lauter trunkener Mund von Geist, das ist Scham, ich tat es nicht ruhig, Scham, ich röhrte und lachte und schrie einige

loud drunken mouth of a mind, that is shame, I didn't do it quietly, shame, I roared and laughed and shouted some drunken thing, I might have sneered Ich bin der Geist der stets verneint but I was only hands and swollen lungs and fat and had no power to do anything always, but just this once I was the power that I was trying to deny. I met the Denying Force, and instead of resisting it or neutralizing it, I let it take me over, I channeled it, let it run through me, a lens. Shame is being a lens for a greater power. Wanton. Shame. Unhealable wound. The white tree I tore up set its roots in me, the white shame tree grows in me. When I come to die, the autopsy will find a white tree inside me, growing through my chest, shame is my tree. Now the horse-psychiatrist who knows so many interesting things will look at me and say, You know, this business of killing a tree, that's not so terrible, people do a lot of worse things than that. And people cut down trees every day, shoot deer, boil lobsters, step on worms, what's the big fuss? Isn't it more likely that all this affect is displaced from some other event, some repressed thing you really did or really happened to you, some repressed site in your psyche, transferred to this stupid tree scenario? Who cares about a tree? Let's get at the real problem, the real thing you're ashamed of. What comes into your mind when I say that? Doctor, you weren't there. You didn't feel the grossness of my feelings. Sullen resentment. Show-off bullying, picking on the only thing I could master. And even that wasn't easy. You didn't see how I struggled to uproot the tree, I was showing off my strength, I have no strength, it was just a

betrunkene Sachen, ich hätte höhnen können *Ich bin der Geist der stets verneint,* aber ich war nur Hände und geschwollene Lungen und Fett und ich hatte immerzu keine Kraft, irgendwas zu tun, doch dieses eine Mal war ich die Kraft, die ich zu verneinen versuchte. Ich traf die Verneinende Macht, und statt ihr zu widerstehen oder sie zu neutralisieren, hiess ich sie mich übernehmen, liess sie durch mich rinnen, rieseln, selbst eine Linse. Scham ist Linse sein für eine grössere Macht. Mutwillig. Scham. Unheilbare Wunde. Der weisse Baum, den ich ausriss, pflanzte seine Wurzeln in mich, der weisse Schambaum wächst in mir. Wenn ich gestorben bin, wird die Autopsie einen weissen Baum in mir finden, der durch meine Brust wächst, Scham ist mein Baum. Nun wird der Pferdepsychiater, der so viele interessante Dinge weiss, mich ansehen und sagen Wissen Sie, diese Sache mit der Baumtöterei, das ist nicht schlimm, Leute tun viel Schlimmeres. Leute holzen jeden Tag Bäume ab, schiessen Wild, kochen Hummer, treten auf Würmer, was solls? Ist es nicht viel wahrscheinlicher, dass alle diese Affekte von einem anderen Vorfall abgezogen werden, etwas Unterdrücktes, was Sie wirklich taten oder was Ihnen wirklich passierte, eine unterdrückte Seite Ihrer Psyche, übertragen auf dieses dümmliche Baumszenario. Wen kümmert ein Baum? Kommen wir zum wirklichen Problem, der wirklichen Sache, für die Sie sich schämen. Was kommt Ihnen in den Sinn? Doktor, Sie waren nicht da. Sie können die Grobheit meiner Gefühle nicht fühlen. Düsterer Groll. Angeberschnickschnack, das einzige Ding in Angriff nehmen, das ich meistern kann. Und selbst das war nicht leicht. Sie haben nicht gesehen, wie

stupid will to hurt, to make my mark, the shame of boasting, the shame of having so little to boast about, doctor, you weren't there, you didn't see the mindlessness, the desire to impress, but there was no one there, the yearning to perform a decisive act, an act that would change my luck. An act that would break the world. And what did I achieve? I killed a tree, and carry shame. The dumbness of it shames me still.

It could have had meaning. Shame is to do something and have no meaning. Shame is to have no meaning, a killed tree lying still brown leafy on the ground and the mother cries. I wounded my life, doctor, the tree is dead and I am dumb with shame, and even when I tell the story I am like a fool, confessing so weird and stupid a crime, even you, doctor, think the real trouble is somewhere else. But it isn't. Shame is a tree. Who knows how long the shadow of the tree falls now, and how much of my life is spoiled by spoiling it? Who knows the reciprocals of things, who knows the shadows? Shame is spoiling a life or a tree, a tree has life, a life has roots and branches and one shameful act seeps through all. Shame is a tree, shame is not knowing where the shadow falls.

Balsam Mountain

ich gerungen habe, um den Baum zu entwurzeln. Ich habe geprotzt mit meiner Kraft, ich habe keine Kraft, es war nur ein dummer Wille, zu verletzen, zu markieren, die Scham, zu prahlen, die Scham, so wenig zum Prahlen zu haben, Doktor, Sie waren nicht da, Sie sahen nicht die Geistlosigkeit, die Begierde, zu beeindrucken, doch da war niemand, die Sehnsucht, einen entscheidenden Akt auszuführen, einen Akt, der mir Glück bringen würde. Ein Akt, der die Welt bricht. Und was habe ich erreicht? Ich tötete einen Baum und trage Scham. Die Stumpfheit davon beschämt mich noch immer.

Es könnte etwas bedeuten. Scham ist, etwas tun und es bedeutet nichts. Scham ist keine Bedeutung haben, ein ermordeter Baum, der noch immer braunbelaubt am Boden liegt, und die Mutter weint. Ich verwundete mein Leben, Doktor, der Baum ist tot und ich bin stumpf vor Scham, und selbst wenn ich die Geschichte erzähle, bin ich ein Narr, ein so krauses und doofes Verbrechen zu bekennen, selbst Sie, Doktor, Sie denken, das wirkliche Problem sei woanders. Aber das ist es nicht. Scham ist ein Baum. Wer weiss schon, wie lang der Schatten des Baumes fällt, und wie viel von meinem Leben verdorben ist, indem ich ihn verdarb. Wer weiss schon von der Umkehrbarkeit der Dinge, wer weiss schon von den Schatten? Scham ist, einen Baum oder ein Leben verschwenden, ein Baum hat Leben, ein Leben hat Wurzeln und Äste und ein schamvoller Akt sickert durch alles. Scham ist ein Baum, Scham ist nicht wissen, wohin der Schatten fällt.

Balsam Mountain

Maybe your shame is a naked tree, neglected naked tree in the middle of the body of your soul, so to say, dear little self, erected soul like a snake vers le ciel, in some red desert, attending you, excited. *Wild monkey, said the Mongolian giant to me, word world monkey, I understood in these woods, when I went through the hole in the wall, to enter the party in the middle of the forbidden heart of the park, I never deny the monkey again. I promise.* I am ashamed of all the promises I gave. I am ashamed to speak poorly in your language. *I want to leave language immediately. I would rather prefer to be a leaf and you the white tree. Language is some sort of killing me.* I want to be decaptured. I want to get out of this much too solid destiny. I want so much tenderness. False. It is a giant power that you want to be released. You are in transit. Correct. They sit in Ireland and steer you through your hard drive. They pack your machines in lilac airmail packets and carry them to Weiterstadt. They cut your hair. They recommend moisturizing. They touch your feet with clay. They tap your knee with their knuckles. They stand you upright. They change your eyeglasses. You are ashamed because they talk about suicide when they look at you. You are ashamed of their anxiety about loving you, their fear of going crazy by doing so. You are ashamed that they betray you and don't keep any of their promises, you are ashamed that they fail you so.

To be a gate for what happens. A fool. A foolish woman.

Maybe your shame is a naked tree, neglected naked tree in the middle of the body of your soul, so to say, dear little self, erected soul like a snake vers le ciel, in some red desert, attending you, in Aufregung. Wild monkey, said the Mongolian giant to me, word world monkey, I understood in these woods, when I went through the hole in the wall, to enter the party in the middle of the forbidden heart of the park. I never deny the monkey again. I promise. Ich schäme mich für alle Versprechen, die ich gab. Ich schäme mich, schlecht in deiner Sprache zu sprechen. I want to leave language immediately. I would rather prefer to be a leaf and you the white tree. Language is some sort of killing me. Ich will entobert sein. Ich will aus dieser viel zu festen Bestimmung. Ich wünsche so viel Zartes. Falsch. Es ist eine Riesenkraft, die du entfesseln willst. Du bist im Transit. Richtig. Sie sitzen in Irland und navigieren dich durch deine Speicher. Sie packen deine Maschinen in lila Luftpakete und tragen sie nach Weiterstadt. Sie schneiden deine Haare. Sie empfehlen dir Feuchtigkeit. Sie berühren deine Füsse mit Lehm. Sie klopfen deine Knie mit den Knöcheln. Sie stellen dich hin. Sie wechseln deine Brille aus. Du schämst dich, dass sie von Selbstmord reden, wenn sie dich sehen. Du schämst dich für ihre Angst, dich zu lieben, ihre Angst, verrückt zu werden dabei. Du schämst dich, dass sie dich verraten und alles, was sie versprechen, nicht halten, du schämst dich, dass sie so scheitern an dir.

Destruction can happen. The gate is action. We are asserted matter. Crowned with this precious stupid ball. Hold me raven tight. You float between my hands, they hold you by your ears. You spell my back, now I love language precise as vertebrae. We are locked together with lines and actions. We are set free. Unbound. A much too close long distance mixture, hotcold, that's what we are. *The Chinese poet renames me in the middle of Beijing, while fishing, yes, renaming is white fishing, while fishing little folded paper ships with candles out of the lake, under the roof of our night boat, to feed the nice floating* with cock and hen for luck on the bow. Later someone would write an e-mail: The cock crows and thereby ushers in his betrayal, as if the betrayal were the whole meaning between the two of you. *Here we are.* You are the chicken. We get wet. *We both like laughing with Kafka. Do you like that? I don't want to get excited. We decide to be brother and sister. Your name is Birdy, he says, I know you.* What I already knew long ago, I know now through you. I knew it in the air, and over the desert, and as it circulated all the birds knew it, there are birds that know everything, and now me. I am shamanized. I am ashamed of the baptism in Beijing. I am ashamed of my loss of virginity above the lake in Ticino.

Always specialities. I am ashamed to be so madly touchable, out of all measure. *Touch me, I beg.* I am inconsolable. I want you to touch me right away for this eternity. I beg the leaf, before it falls, to brush against me when it does.

Ein Tor sein für das, was passiert, ein Thor. Eine Thörin. Zerstören kann passieren. Das Tor ist Tat. Wir sind behaupteter Stoff. Gekrönt mit dieser köstlich blöden Kugel. Halt mich Raben fest. Du schwebst zwischen meinen Händen an den Ohren. Du buchstabierst meinen Rücken, jetzt liebe ich die Sprache fest wie Wirbel. Wir sind aus Zeilen und Taten zusammengesperrt. Wir sind losgemacht. Entbunden. Ein viel zu nahes Ferngemisch heisskalt sind wir. The Chinese poet renames me in the middle of Bejing, while fishing, yes renaming is white fishing, while fishing little folded paper ships with candles out of the lake under the roof of our night boat, to feed the nice floating with Hahn und Henne als Glück am Bug. Später wird jemand mailen: Der Hahn kräht, und damit seinen Verrat einleiten, als sei der Verrat der ganze Sinn zwischen euch. Here we are. Du bist das Huhn. Wir werden nass. We both like laughing with Kafka. Do you like that? I dont want to get excited. We decide to be brother and sister. Your name is Birdy, he says, I know you. Was ich schon viel vorher weiss, weiss ich jetzt durch dich. Ich wusste es in der Luft, davor und über der Wüste, und wie es zirkulierte, wussten es alle Vögel, es sind Vögel, die das alles wissen, jetzt ich. Ich bin schamanisiert. Ich schäme mich für die Taufe in Bejing. Ich schäme mich für die Entjungferung über dem See im Tessin.

Immer Spezialitäten. Ich schäme mich, so verrückt ausser der Ordnung berührbar zu sein. Touch me, I beg. Ich bin untröstlich. Ich will sofort, dass du mich berührst nach dieser Ewigkeit. Ich bitte das Blatt, bevor es fällt, mich zu streifen dabei.

I beg the sky. The street. I look you in the eyes and beg you to touch me, who has travelled into you in double time and the speed of light by herself. I hate it having to hang around lost in everything. Not being summoned to you, not being called back to you, to be unloved, unbodied, suicided, with two heads pointing in different directions, that is nakeder than naked, that is nothingness. I am ashamed to be nothing. Naturally I am ashamed to beg you so relentlessly to hold me and to sit down crying on your bed, till you lay your belly on my back, that arches back till I'm on my knees in a hotel in Shanghai. I am in an immense getting ready with you, that goes on even when we drop out. Don't drop out. I cry, I stamp my feet, I write, I strive for embodiment. I want us to be bodies together in the interim. I would rather be healthy. Light and healthy with myself and light and like that with you, who is healthy and maybe dark, heavy, or smolders. I would rather be Birdy, I hear it as *bei dir*, with you in Beijing, in a little boat on the lake, not this monster flower that I see grieving in me, *mourning*. Shame is the crack. Swollen. A yapping. Greed. I am ashamed of not embracing you and forgetting myself, ashamed of ensnaring you so cunningly, ashamed of hiding you away. I am ashamed that you will be reading this soon, and you too, that we collaborate so far beyond ourselves, and that it's not personal, but is true. And it will be true and it was true and that, before it passes, it gets written down. What a wandering place I am, what a standing stone.

Ich bitte den Himmel. Die Strasse. Ich bitte dich mitten in die Augen, mich zu berühren, die in dich gefahren ist mit Sauseschritt und Lichtgeschwindigkeit von selbst. Ich hasse es draussen verloren herumzuhängen im All. Nicht an dich herangeholt, nicht in dich zurückgerufen, nämlich entliebt zu sein, klassisch entleibt, mit doppeltem Kopf in zwiefache Richtung, das ist nackter als nackt, das ist Nichts. Ich schäme mich, nicht zu sein. Ich schäme mich natürlich, dich so unerbittlich anzubetteln, mich anzufassen, und weinend auf deinem Bett zu sitzen, bis du deinen Bauch auf meinen Rücken legst, der sich auf meine Knie krümmt in einem Hotel in Shanghai. Ich bin in einer immensen Vorbereitung mit dir, die weiter geht, auch wenn wir aussteigen. Steig nicht aus. Ich weine, ich stampfe, ich schreibe, ich suche Verkörperung. Ich will, dass wir zusammen Körper sind im Übergang. Ich wäre lieber heil. Leicht und heil mit mir selbst und licht und so mit dir, der heil und vielleicht dunkel ist, schwer, oder brennt. Ich wäre lieber Birdy, ich höre: bei dir, in Bejing, im Boot auf dem See, nicht diese Monsterblume, die ich in mir grollen seh, mourning. Die Scham ist der Riss. Ein Schwulst. Ein grobes Geklaffe. Eine Gier. Ich schäme mich, dich nicht in Selbstvergessenheit zu umarmen, dich raffiniert zu umgarnen und zu verstecken. Ich schäme mich, dass du dies bald liest, und du auch, dass wir weit ausserhalb von uns kollabieren und dass es nicht persönlich ist, aber wahr. Und sein wird und wahr war und dass es, bevor es passiert, aufgeschrieben ist. Was für eine Wanderstelle, was für eine Stele bin ich.

Ich schäme mich, weil «du» immer der Name von wem anders
ist. Jemand, den ich immer kennen will. Berühren scheint
immer der Weg zu jemand zu sein. Es scheint fast zu genügen.
Die Haut sagt: Die Haut ist alles. Das Berühren sagt: Ich
genüge. Die Haut sagt: Ich bin deine Nationalität, ich bin
deine Politik. Ich schäme mich, dass Berühren genug ist. Ist es
immer Haut? // *Was ist immer?* // Von was ist Haut das
Zeichen? Sie kann nicht nur sie selbst sein, oder? Der
Physiologe sagt: Die Haut ist das grösste Organ im Körper. Na
gut. Organe tun Dinge. Organe arbeiten. Was tut Haut?

Haut reinigt. Genauso Berühren, was immer eine delikate,
köstliche Besudlung zu sein scheint, Berühren reinigt auch.
Weil Berühren zuhört. Alle Sprache berührt sich selbst.
Manchmal schäme ich mich wegen Sprache, wie ich sie höre,
wie ich sie durch das Hören etwas sagen lassen möchte. Ich
denke, auch die Sprache schämt sich für mich, und das ist Teil
des Problems, oder das ganze Problem. Sprache schämt sich
für mich, weil ich sie Dinge sagen lasse, und dann will ich
sofort zu den Dingen, die ich gerade sagte, hingehen und sie
anfassen. Das ist Krieg. Der ewige Streit zwischen dem Ding
und seinem Namen, durch Berühren gelöst. Ich schäme mich,
dass ich, wenn ich einen Text lese und er sagt: «Berühr mich»,
denke, es sagt mir, dass ich jeden berühren soll, der diese
Worte sagt. «Fass mich an.» Es macht, dass ich dich berühren
will, wer immer du bist, zu wem immer du sprichst. // *Was
immer hier immer ist.* // Hören mischt sich ein. Mein Hören

SHAME 8

I am ashamed because "you" is always the name of someone
else. Someone I always want to know. Touch always seems
to be the way to someone. It seems almost to satisfy. The
skin says: The skin is all. The touch says: I am enough. Skin
says: I am your nationality, I am your politics. I am ashamed
that touch is enough. Is it always skin? What is skin the sign
of? It can't be just itself, can it? The physiologists say: The
skin is the largest organ in the body. Well, then. Organs do
things. Organs work. What does skin do?

Skin purifies. So touch, which always seems to be a delicate,
delicious defilement, touch also purifies. Because touch
listens. All language touches itself. Sometimes I am
ashamed of language, because of how I hear it, of how I
want to make it mean by listening. I think language also is
ashamed of me, and that is part of the problem, or the
whole problem. Language is ashamed of me because I let it
say things and then I want to go right up to the things that I
have just said, go up and touch them. This is war. The
eternal strife between the thing and its name, solved by
touch. I am ashamed because when I read a text and it says
"Touch me," I think it is telling me to touch whoever says
the words. It makes me want to touch you, whoever you are,
whoever you are talking to. Hearing interferes. My hearing
you interferes with the work of language, I am ashamed, I
butt in, I put myself in the place of The One To Whom You
Are Speaking. I am ashamed of this intrusion. To hear

mischt sich in die Arbeit der Sprache, ich schäme mich, ich platze rein, ich setz mich an die Stelle des einen, zu dem du sprichst. Ich schäme mich für diese Störung. Sie sprechen hören, heisst auch, in ihren Raum eindringen. Ihre Worte, ihr kaum gehaltenes Schweigen, gibt dir eine Öffnung. Das ist Invasion.

Aber wenn ich dich sagen höre: «berühr mich», fühle ich überhaupt keine Scham, ich erhebe mich und eile durch die Sprache zu dem Platz, wo Sprache endet. Es strömt über deine Haut, wie der Rhein in Schaffhausen sich gewaltig über die Felskante spreizt runter nach Europa, von den Bergen. Alle Berge der Welt sind dasselbe Land, ein anderer Kontinent, die harte Luft, der Irrsinn, der im Himmel fixiert ist.

Sprache quillt über über alles. Ich schäme mich für mich selbst, weil die Sprache nie endet. Wenn sie enden würde, oder wenn ich nur einmal aufhören könnte, zuzuhören, dann wäre sie mal der laute Fluss, mal die Stille vom heiligen Wald. Ich wäre verloren in diesen Wäldern und würde mich nie mehr schämen. Gerade jetzt schäme ich mich, nicht verloren zu sein. Ich weiss, wo ich bin und wo du wahrscheinlich bist. Ich bin so bewegt durch das, was du mir sagst. Doch, bist du es? Und sagst du es, und bin ich es, dem du es sagst? Und wer bin ich? Wer, denkst du, bin ich, wenn du dich schämst, dass ich lesen werde, was du denkst, und wenn ich denken werde, was du sagst, und ich werde nur einen kleinen Teil von dem sagen, was ich meine?

someone talking is also to invade their space. Their words, their ill-kept silence, give you an opening. This is invasion.

But when I hear you say "touch me" I feel no shame at all, I rise up and hurry through language to the place where language ends. It spills out on your skin, like the Rhine at Schaffhausen splaying out huge over the rock ledges down into Europe, from the mountains. All the mountains in the world are the same country, another continent, the hard air, the madness fixed in the sky.

Language spills over everything, I am ashamed of myself because language never ends. If it ended, or if I could for once stop listening, then it would be sometimes the noisy river, sometimes the silence of the Holy Forest. I would be lost in those woods and never be ashamed. Right now I am ashamed not to be lost. I know where I am, and where you probably are. I am so moved by what you tell me. But is it you? And are you telling, and is it me you're telling? And who am I? Who do you think I am when you are ashamed that I will read what you're thinking and I will think what you're saying and I will say only a small part of what I mean?

You will think: He is ashamed, that is who he really is.

But I know too much to be ashamed. Really, I am ashamed of knowing so much. Where can I touch you? I am ashamed of where the words don't tell me, ashamed of where I wait

Er schämt sich, wirst du denken, das ist, wer er wirklich ist.

Doch ich weiss zuviel, um mich zu schämen. Wirklich, ich schäme mich, so viel zu wissen. Wo kann ich dich anfassen? Ich schäme mich da, wo die Worte es mir nicht sagen, schäme mich, wo ich ungewiss warte. *Insel. Brücke. Hand.* Ich weiss die Hand, Hand ist *honte*, Hand ist Scham, ich schäme mich für meine Hände, wieviel sie anfassen. Hand hört sich an wie Hund, Jagdhund, Jagen, Spuken, was Phantome tun, *Gespenster, Gewitter*, ich schäme mich für das Wetter, das mein Leben bestimmt, die Regenstürme, von denen nur blasse *Feuchtigkeit* bleibt, traurige Moisture in der Mitte des Herzens. Gibt es so was wie Herz wirklich? Ich schäme mich für die herzlosen Begierden, die mein Leben jagen. Ich schaue beschämt hoch von deinem Text. Warum habe ich so lange gewartet? Was will ich von diesen Worten, die ich gelesen habe? Ich will etwas von ihnen, was sie von mir wollen, oder auch nicht. Was wollen Worte, wenn sie in der Nacht des Briefumschlags murmeln, dem Wald des Buches, auf dem Bildschirm glimmen, den du vergessen hast auszuschalten? Ich schäme mich dafür, mehr zu wollen. Ist der Text nicht genug? Wenn ein Mann die Bibel liest, muss es einen Gott geben, oder wenigstens einen Engel, die ausserhalb des Buches auf ihn warten, so, dass Er da ist, wenn er das Buch schliesst. Ist das Buch nicht genug? In meiner Bibel mache ich Leute. Ich studiere sie, glaube an sie und bete zu ihnen. Wenn sie antworten, bin ich wahrhaftig gesegnet. Es ist wieder dieses Wort «du», die heiligen zwei Buchstaben, die in der Bibel leben und zu mir nachts von jedem anderen Buch sprechen.

uncertain. Insel. Brücke. Hand. I know hand, hand is *honte*, hand is shame, I am ashamed of my hands, how much they touch. Hand sounds like haunt, what phantoms do, Gespenster, Gewitter, I am ashamed of the weather that runs my life, the rainstorms from which only pale Feuchtigkeit is left, sad moisture in the middle of the heart. Is there such a thing as a heart, really? I am ashamed of heartless desires that haunt my life. I look up ashamed from reading your text. Why have I waited so long? What do I want from these words I've read? I want something from them they may or may not want from me. What do words want, murmuring in the night of the envelope, the forest of the book, glimmering on the monitor you forgot to turn off? I am ashamed of wanting more. Isn't the text enough? When a man reads the Bible, does there have to be a God or at least an angel standing waiting for him just outside the book, so He's there when he closes the pages? Isn't the book enough? I make people into my Bible. I study them and believe in them and pray to them. When they answer, yea verily I am blessed. It is that word "you" again, the holy Triliteral that lives in the Bible and speaks to me at night from every other book. I have been brought to be ashamed of wanting people to be my Bible, of worshipping only what I can touch.

Shame is a country too. A narrow corridor between Portugal and Spain, hot sun, cold wind, black sand. Shameland. Your glasses slip down your nose, I reach out and gently push them back up the bridge. Your lenses are

Ich bin dazu gebracht worden, mich dafür zu schämen, zu wünschen, dass Menschen meine Bibel sind, und nur das anzubeten, was ich anfassen kann.

Scham ist auch ein Land. Ein schmaler Korridor zwischen Portugal und Spanien, heisse Sonne, kalter Wind, schwarzer Sand. Schamland. Deine Brille rutscht von deiner Nase, ich streck die Hand aus und stupse sie zart zurück über den Nasenrücken. Deine Brillengläser sind mit Wassertropfen gesprenkelt. Die See ist nah. Ich kann kaum dein Gesicht sehen im Gegenlicht. Die Sonne geht unter, der Sand ist schwarz. Wenn wir lang genug warten, kann ich dich besser sehen. Deine Worte haben mich sehr bewegt, wie sie aus der Zeit herauskamen, aus China, aus einer anderen Sprache, wie sie zu mir kamen und mich nicht meinten. Meinten mich und gingen weit. Meinten etwas, was durch mich durch passierte, mich berührte, als es passierte, auf dem Weg zu wem, den du meinst. Es gibt so viele Wege für die Worte, ihre bizarre Bestimmung zu erfüllen. Worte berühren wie Diebe auf dem Marktplatz.

Oder später, in der Dunkelheit, glaube ich, du erinnerst dich an Dinge, die du geschrieben hast, und ich denke, ich höre dich sie wieder sagen. Und so versuche ich nun zu antworten. Jede Frage schlägt die Art und Weise ihrer Antwort vor. Ich möchte deinen Worten mit deinen Worten antworten, aber ich habe nur die Worte, die deine Worte meine Worte in meiner Sprache passieren lassen und auf diese Weise in mir passieren. Jemandem zuhören ist immer Dialog. Das Spiel,

dimpled with water drops. The sea is near. I can barely see your face against the sun glare. The sun is setting, the sand is black. If we can wait long enough, I will see you better. Your words moved me so much, coming out of time, out of China, out of another language, coming to me, and not meaning me. Meaning me and going far. Meaning something that passed right through me, touching me as it passed, on its way to the one you mean. So many ways the words have of fulfilling their bizarre destiny. Words touch like thieves in a marketplace.

Or later, in darkness, I think you remember things you wrote, and I think I hear you say them again. And so I try to answer. Every question proposes the terms and conditions of its answer. I want to answer your words with your words, but I have only the words your words make happen in my language, and in that way make happen in me. So listening to someone is always a dialogue. The play the trauerspiel the tragedy the comedy the farce the entertainment the passion play the pageant—the play is the form beneath and before poetry and fiction, it is language listening to itself and answering inside itself the consequences of the words it hears. I must insist that this interior responding is inescapable, inflexible. It happens when anyone speaks. And so the play begins, which is not different from hearing you say:

B: I waited *in the middle of the forbidden part of the park.*

das *Trauerspiel*, die Tragödie, die Komödie, die Farce, die Unterhaltung, das Passionsspiel, das Festspiel, das Spiel ist vor und unterhalb von Dichtung und Fiktion, die Sprache, die sich selbst zuhört und in sich selbst den Konsequenzen der Worte antwortet, die sie hört. Ich muss darauf bestehen, dieses innere Beantworten ist unausweichlich, unerbittlich. Es passiert, egal wer spricht. Und so beginnt das Spiel, was nichts anderes ist, als dich sagen hören:

B: Ich wartete *in der Mitte des verbotenen Teils des Parks.*

R: Ich weiss. Das ist der Park, in den ich oft gehe und die Krähen beobachte, wie sie den Himmel aufribbeln und die Nacht durchfallen lassen. Der Park ist das Zentrum der alten Stadt, der Hauptstadt von Schamland. Ich besuche den Park oft, Zwielicht, Dämmerung. Meist schau ich in den Himmel. Manchmal sitz ich einfach da und spiele Schach mit Fremden. Als Partner wähle ich mir die, deren Schachfiguren rot und schwarz sind, nicht schwarz und weiss. Manchmal sitze ich einfach und beobachte die Leute, die nicht du sind, vorbei spazieren. In ihren eigenen Leben sind diese Leute natürlich auch du, aber das hilft mir nicht. Es tröstet. Ich war im Park, ich habe auch gewartet. Es scheint mir, dass ich immer gewartet habe. Ich habe mich geschämt, beim Warten gesehen zu werden, ich schäme mich, dass du warten musstest.

Es gibt so viel Warten. Die Welt sollte sich schämen. Die Dinge sind alle da, die ganze Zeit, weil es Sprache gibt. Dinge sind nicht weiter weg als Worte, oder? Doch warum ist

R: I know. This is the park I often walk in, watching the crows unknit the sky and let the night fall through. The park is in the center of the old city, capital of Shameland. I visit the park often, twilight, crepuscule. Mostly I look at the sky. Sometimes I just sit and play chess with strangers. I choose for partners those whose chessmen are red and black, rather than black and white. Sometimes I just sit and watch all the people who aren't you come walking by. In their own lives, of course, these people are also you, but that doesn't help me. It consoles. I was there in the park, I was waiting too. It seems to me I have always been waiting. I was ashamed to be seen waiting, I am ashamed that you had to wait.

There is so much waiting. The world should be ashamed! Because things are right here all the time, because language is. Things are no further away than words, are they? But why is any part of the park forbidden? Can't we speak in all of them? Is it the little pond where the ducks float and old women and young men in love come down and toss bread to them? This bread is what they've stuffed in their pockets furtively while the Slovenian waitresses aren't watching, the Turkish waitresses, the Portuguese waitresses, the Latvian waitresses in the cheap hotel young men in love always stay in, cramming food into their mouths for a breakfast that has to last them the whole day, plus extra bread and rolls for the ducks, you can't be in love without feeding the whole world. Is that what is forbidden? Are you a woman in love, who must shun the gloomy duck ponds where young louts sob?

irgendein Teil dieses Parks verboten? Können wir nicht in allen Teilen sprechen? Ist es der kleine Teich, wo die Enten schwimmen, zu dem alte Frauen und junge verliebte Männer kommen und ihnen Brot zuwerfen? Das Brot, das sie heimlich in ihre Taschen stopften, während die slowenischen Kellnerinnen nicht aufpassten, die portugiesischen Kellnerinnen, die türkischen Kellnerinnen, die lettischen Kellnerinnen in den billigen Hotels, in denen sich verliebte junge Männer immer aufhalten und Frühstück in ihre Münder stopfen, das den ganzen Tag halten muss, plus extra Brot und Brötchen für die Enten, du kannst nicht verliebt sein, ohne die ganze Welt zu füttern. Ist es das, was verboten ist? Bist du eine verliebte Frau, die den dunklen Ententeich meiden muss, wo die jungen Rüpel schluchzen?

B: *Ich schäme mich, deine Sprache schlecht zu sprechen. Ich will sofort Sprache haben.*

R: Das Gefühl hab ich auch, ich kenne es sehr. Ich kenne dein Gefühl, dieses Wissen ohne Sprechen. Ich kann überhaupt keine Sprache sprechen. Was sie meine nennen, ist am wenigsten meine. Meine Muttersprache habe ich nie gelernt. Ich schäme mich, nicht sprechen zu können. Das ist die Wurzel all meiner Scham. Sie sagen: Sag etwas. Sprich zu den Leuten. Sprich. Sie sagen: Zuhause liest er immer Bücher und nun sagt er kein Wort, was ist los, hat die Katze deine Zunge? Die Katze hatte meine Zunge. Sie rannte weg mit meiner Zunge und nahm sie als ihre. Ich schäme mich, dass die Katze meine Zunge hat, hat sie und spricht nicht, sie macht

B: *I'm ashamed to speak your language badly. I want to have language immediately.*

R: The feeling is mine, I know it so keenly. I know your feeling, this knowing without speaking. I can't speak any language. What they call my own is least my own. My mother tongue is what I never learned. I am ashamed of not being able to speak. That is the root of all my shame. They would say: Say something! Talk to people! Speak! They would say, At home he's always reading books, and now he doesn't say a word, what's the matter, does the cat have your tongue? The cat had my tongue. He ran with my tongue and took it for his own. I am ashamed because the cat has my tongue, has it and it doesn't speak, he makes mewing sounds but his tongue is only for licking. My tongue is wet. I lick but I don't speak. I am ashamed of being so languageless. I have a voice but I cannot speak. Because I have no language. Even, I have no shame. I am ashamed of having no shame, of being so shameless. Wordlessness is shame. To have nothing to say for yourself. The cat has my tongue, I speak only foreign languages, very badly. I speak Cat.

B: *Language is … sort of killing me too.*

R: It's the park that's killing us, the Irish green and the huge silos jutting into the sky, sometimes the grain ferments and pressure builds up inside them, they explode, they shoot into the sky like rockets, Raketenspeicher, full of exploding

Miaugeräusche, doch ihre Zunge ist nur fürs Lecken. Meine Zunge ist nass. Ich lecke, aber spreche nicht. Ich schäme mich, so sprachlos zu sein. Ich habe eine Stimme, aber kann nicht sprechen. Weil ich keine Sprache habe. Nicht mal Scham. Ich schäme mich, keine Scham zu haben, so schamlos zu sein. Wortlosigkeit ist Scham. Selbst nichts zu sagen haben. Die Katze hat meine Zunge, ich spreche nur fremde Sprachen, sehr schlecht. Ich spreche Katze.

B: *Die Sprache tötet mich … auch irgendwie.*

R: Es ist der Park, der uns tötet, das irische Grün und die grossen Silos, die in den Himmel ragen, manchmal fermentieren die Samen und Druck baut sich innen auf, sie explodieren, sie schiessen in den Himmel wie Raketen, *Raketenspeicher*, voll mit explosivem Gas, der Park tötet uns, das herbe Eden, das Paradies der leeren Pariser und verdorbenen Mittagessen, Sekretärinnen, die halbnackt im Gras am Eisbach sitzen, Velofahrer, die in Briefkästen crashen und stürzen, stürzen, die Räder drehen leer, die Trumpfkarten vom Tarot wirbeln durch die Luft wie die Frontseiten von Zeitungen, in Sprachen, die du nicht lesen kannst, ich kann jede Sprache lesen, alles sagt dasselbe. Der Park ist verboten, weil darin Vergnügen ist, die Enten warten auf ihr Futter, die jungen Männer schluchzen und kneten die weichen weissen Krümel von kleinen *Brötchen* und werfen sie in die flachen offenen Schnäbel der Vögel. Jedesmal, wenn eine Ente mit Schnabel in der Luft einen Krumen fängt, bevor das Brot ins Wasser fällt, denkt der junge Mann, die Frau, in die er verliebt

gas, the park is killing us, the sour Eden, the Paradise of empty condoms and spoiled lunchtimes, secretaries sitting half naked on the grass by the Eisbach, cyclists crashing into post boxes and falling, falling, wheels spinning, the Trump cards of the Tarot whirling through the air like the front pages of newspapers in languages you can't read, I can read every language, it all says the same thing. The park is forbidden because there is pleasure there, the ducks are waiting for their chow, the young men sob and finger the soft white crumb of little brötchen, toss them to the flat open beaks of the birds. Each time a duck catches a crumb with its bill in the air, before the bread hits the water, then the young man thinks it means the woman he loves will love him. For a moment or two he sobs a little less, and throws more bread. The secretaries on the grass, almost naked now in the strong spring sunlight, laugh at all these young men. How can you be in love when there are so many? Touch me. Their very smooth skin underneath the knees.

B: *They recommend humidity, they suggest that you be wet.*

R: They recommended some kind of moisture, who knows what. They said I was made of clay and should always keep myself wet. Otherwise, otherwise I'd dry out and bake and crack. I would be a piece of china. They said I was made from clay, a rabbi took clay and shaped it, put a special word on a piece of paper and put it in my mouth. Immediately I began to move around. I have to keep wet. Heraclitus, on

ist, wird ihn lieben. Für einen Moment oder zwei schluchzt er etwas weniger und wirft mehr Brot. Die Sekretärinnen im Gras, fast nackt im starken Frühlingssommerlicht, lachen über diese jungen Männer. Wie kannst du dich verlieben, wenn es so viele gibt. Berühr mich. Ihre sehr weiche Haut unter den Knien.

B: *Sie empfehlen Feuchtigkeit, sie schlagen vor, dass du nass bist.*

R: Sie empfehlen irgendeine Art Feuchtigkeit, wer weiss was. Sie sagten, ich sei aus Lehm gemacht und soll mich immer feucht halten. Sonst würde ich austrocknen und backen und krachen. Ich würde zu einem Stück Porzellan. Sie sagten, ein Rabiner habe Lehm genommen, mich geformt, ein spezielles Wort auf ein Stück Papier geschrieben und mir in den Mund geschoben. Sofort habe ich mich bewegt. Ich muss mich nass halten. Heraklit erklärt dagegen: Es ist der Tod für die Seele, nass zu sein. Vielleicht hat die Nässe meine Seele aufgelöst. Doch ich kann mich immer noch bewegen und Dinge tun. Ich kann nicht sprechen, ich habe dieses Papierstück in meinem Mund. Es steht nur ein Wort darauf geschrieben, das einzige Wort, das jemals in meinem Mund ist, aber ich kann es nicht aussprechen. Meine Zunge kann nicht lesen. Ich bin ein Monster. Berühr mich.

B: Dann *kommen sie* und *wechseln deine Brille aus.*

R: Nun kann ich sehen. Ich bin jemand anders, ich sehe das jetzt. Kein Monster, aber berühr mich trotzdem. Eine

the contrary, explains: It is death for the soul to be wet. Perhaps the wetness dissolved my soul. But I can still move and do things. I can't talk, I have this piece of paper in my mouth. It has only one word written on it, the only word that's ever in my mouth, but I can't pronounce it. My tongue can't read. I am a monster. Touch me.

B: Then *they come* and *change your eyeglasses.*

R: Now I can see. I am someone else, I see that now. Not a monster, but touch me anyhow. An obsession is an obsession, you can't get rid of one just by changing your name or gender or identity. I carry it with me, all of it, shame by shame, like a wife at a picnic unpacking the lunch basket, pickles and cheeses and ham and bottles and mustard and salt and oil and pepper, one after another, salad and crackers, shame by shame, each one, ashamed of my body, ashamed of my mind, ashamed of my desires, ashamed of what I don't do, ashamed of what I've done, cheeses and salami and touch me, wine and Gerolsteiner and napkins and all the people I hurt, I am ashamed of hurting so many, of being hurt, of touching, of wanting to touch. I am ashamed of touching. I couldn't talk so I had to touch. I couldn't see well, I had no glasses, no see, must touch. A thing was real only when I felt it in my hands. The yielding flesh of it. Its breath on my face. Not being able to see made me see inside instead. Inner vision only heals by touch. When they said to me in those days: Say something! all I could do was see pictures in my head. Say something.

Obsession ist eine Obsession, du kannst sie nicht loswerden, indem du deinen Namen änderst oder dein Geschlecht oder deine Identität. Ich trage es mit mir, alles, Scham für Scham, wie eine Frau beim Picknick den Korb auspackt, Gurken und Käse und Schinken und Flaschen und Senf und Salz und Öl und Pfeffer, eins nach dem anderen, Salat und Crackers, Scham für Scham, jedes einzelne, Scham wegen meinem Körper, Scham wegen meinem Geist, Scham, wegen meiner Begierde, Scham wegen dem, was ich nicht tu, Scham wegen dem, was ich tat, Käse und Salami, und berühr mich, Wein und Gerolsteiner und Tischdecken und die Leute, die ich verletzte, ich schäme mich, so viele verletzt zu haben, verletzt zu sein, zu berühren, berühren zu wollen. Ich schäme mich fürs Berühren. Ich konnte nicht reden, also musste ich berühren. Ich konnte nicht gut sehen, ich hatte keine Brille, nicht sehen, muss anfassen. Eine Sache war nur real, wenn ich sie in meinen Händen fühlen konnte. Ihr gefügiges Fleisch. Ihr Atem in meinem Gesicht. Die Unfähigkeit zu sehen liess mich dafür innen sehen. Innere Vision heilt nur durch Berührung. Als sie in jenen Tagen zu mir sagten: Sag etwas! konnte ich nur Bilder sehen in meinem Kopf, das war alles. Sag etwas. Sieh etwas. Sag etwas. Sieh etwas. Sieh Bilder von dort, wo ich wirklich sein wollte, mit wem oder allein, und was tun. Diese Bilder füllten meinen Kopf und verstopften ihn. Keine Worte für all diese Bilder. Ein Bild zerstört tausend Worte. Selbst mit Brille kann ich die Sätze nicht sagen, die ich sehe. Worte verstecken sich innen in ihrer Bedeutung, eure Namen sind in Bildern versteckt. Ich versuche in Richtung irgendeiner Tür zu stolpern, was ich mit irgend etwas zu

See something. Say something. See something. See pictures of where I really wanted to be, with whom or alone, doing what. Those images filled my head and choked. No words for all those images. One picture destroys a thousand words. And even with eyeglasses I can't say the sentence I see. Words hide inside their meanings, your names hide in images. I try to stumble towards some door I confuse with saying something. I feel I have to know the right words to open it.

B: But *the gate is deed*. Not saying but doing. I fly from you.

R: You fly from me because the crows are screaming every morning, they are ashamed at how little I leave them every night, an opera here, an opera there, a book left in the snow. An opossum waddles under the porch with something in its mouth, I am ashamed of how little I feed the world, no wonder you fly away, you give me so much and I give you so little. I am ashamed of how little I give you. Even when I touch you this touch is something I am taking from you. A touch takes. But when someone touches me, that is someone giving to me, so no matter what happens, I am always taking and hardly giving, like a coast with no fjords, all storms, no harbors, I give so little, I am ashamed.

B: But you have learned how to *spell my back*.

R: That is how fingers take, vertebra by vertebra, the letters of your secret name. The name of anyone is his spine. Too

sagen verwechsle. Ich fühle es, ich muss die richtigen Worte wissen, um sie zu öffnen.

B: Doch *Tor ist Tat*. Nicht sagen, doch Tun. Ich fliehe dich.

R: Du fliehst mich, weil die Krähen jeden Morgen kreischen, sie schämen sich, wie wenig ich ihnen jede Nacht lasse, eine Oper hier, eine Oper da, ein Buch im Schnee. Eine Beutelratte watschelt unter die Veranda mit etwas im Mund, ich schäme mich, wie wenig ich die Welt füttere, kein Wunder, dass du weg fliegst, du gibst mir so viel und ich dir so wenig. Ich schäme mich, wie wenig ich dir gebe. Selbst wenn ich dich berühre, ist dieses Berühren etwas, was ich von dir nehme. Berühren nimmt. Aber wenn jemand mich berührt, gibt er mir etwas, egal was passiert, ich nehme immer und gebe kaum, wie eine Küste mit keinen Fjorden, alles Sturm, kein Hafen, ich gebe so wenig, ich schäme mich.

B: Aber du hast *meinen Rücken buchstabieren* gelernt.

R: So nehmen Finger, Wirbel für Wirbel, die Buchstaben deines geheimen Namens. Der Name von jedem ist seine Wirbelsäule. Zu nah, zu fern, zu fernnah und nahfern, du stellst mich zuhause zurück ins Regal, meine schlammigen Finger hängen herunter und streifen jeden, der vorbeikommt, ich bin eine schmutzige Anwesenheit in deinem sauberen Haus, ein Golem, ich bin von falscher Grösse, immerzu, ich schäme mich, wie gross und klein und nah und fern ich bin. Ich buchstabierte deinen Rücken und lernte mehr als deinen

close, too far, too farclose and nearfar, you put me away on the shelf in your house, my muddy fingers hang down and brush against anyone who passes by, I am a dirty presence in your clean house, a Golem, I am the wrong size, always, I am ashamed of how big and small and near and far I am. I spelled your back and learned more than your name. But when my body tries to pronounce it, you run away. You run all the way to China, where there are poets who stand ankle deep in country dust and drink warm rice wine. Freely. Poets always do what they are supposed to do. Poets are invented by the poems they write, Rimbaud was invented by the little girl whose behind he bit when he was seven years old. We grow from what we grow. A poet turns into what he says. Their Chinese eyes can see the wind and their shoulders in loose robes can feel the friction of the full moon passing. The Chinese poet gives you a new name, you come back and challenge me to spell your new name, you tease me, test me, can I read it from the bones of your back? I put on my new glasses, I lost my virginity in Switzerland, I found it again under a mountain in Donegal, where do you keep things while they're gone?

B: *All the many things I knew before, now I know through you.*

R: And what did he say when you said that? Did he confess that his knowing was enlarged immensely by you? Or did he admit that the old song still held him, das älteste Lied, he heard it before he was born, und immer bläuen licht die Ferne, there is no end, no horizon, the road is an

Namen. Aber wenn mein Körper es auszusprechen versucht, rennst du weg. Du rennst weit weg nach China, wo Dichter knöcheltief in Landstaub stehen und warmen Reiswein trinken. Ungehindert. Dichter tun immer, was sie tun müssen. Dichter werden durch die Gedichte erfunden, die sie schreiben, Rimbaud wurde durch das kleine Mädchen erfunden, deren Hintern er biss, als er sieben Jahre alt war. Wir wachsen durch was wir wachsen lassen. Ein Dichter verwandelt sich in das, was er sagt. Ihre chinesischen Augen können den Wind sehen, und ihre Schultern in den leichten Kleidern können die Reibung des vorbeiziehenden Vollmonds fühlen. Der chinesische Dichter gibt dir einen neuen Namen, du kommst zurück und forderst mich heraus, deinen neuen Namen zu buchstabieren, du neckst mich, testest mich, kann ich es von den Knochen deines Rückens ablesen? Ich zieh meine neue Brille an, ich verlor meine Jungfräulichkeit in der Schweiz, ich fand sie wieder unter einem Berg in Donegal, wo behältst du die Dinge, während sie weg sind?

B: *All die Dinge, die ich vorher wusste, weiss ich jetzt durch dich.*

R: Und was sagte er, als du das sagtest? Hat er zugegeben, dass sich sein Wissen durch dich enorm vergrösserte? Oder gab er zu, dass das alte Lied ihn immer noch hielt, *das älteste Lied*, er hörte es, bevor er geboren wurde, *und immer bläuen licht die Ferne*, das ist kein Ende, kein Horizont, die Strasse ist eine unendliche Agony, die Strasse ist ein dummer Zirkel, hilf mir? Doch wer die Strasse entlang geht, ist immer allein, und das ist schön, schön wie ein westlicher Brotlaib oder ein

interminable agony, the road is a stupid circle, help me? But walking along the road one is always alone, and that is beautiful, beautiful, like a loaf of Western bread or a Chinese peach lying half rotten by the side of the road, and the road doesn't know it.

But when he said that to you, or you said that to him (there is no gender in the I-words, in the you-words, not in German, not in English) what did you think, isn't it the final field mark of being in love, that everything is different now, even the things that aren't different at all?

I am ashamed at saying you all the time. Some people are ashamed of saying I, I, I … but I'm ashamed of saying you this and you that, your this and your that, and always putting you and your into sentences beginning with me. What I feel or what I want. What could a road know anyhow? It goes till it gets there and doesn't even know enough to sleep. But what if it did know? If a road were like a Knight Templar who had fallen, who stretched out in a long dream of dying and men and women and oxen and sheep walked along his body from Istanbul to Cadiz, what would his dream be? What will he tell us when he wakes? His hand clutches a half-eaten peach, juicy, but dust is on the wet fruit. He recommends humidity but is afraid to eat. Wake him. It is stupid just to walk along the road. That is what we must do. Wake the road. And when he wakes, what shame he will feel! Sleeping in public, his back in the air and people on him, his fingers sticky and his head in Spain!

chinesischer Pfirsich, der halb verrottet am Strassenrand liegt, und die Strasse weiss nichts davon.

Aber als er es zu dir sagte, oder du sagtest es zu ihm (es gibt kein Geschlecht in den Ich-Wörtern, in den Du-Wörtern, nicht auf Deutsch, nicht auf Englisch), was dachtest du, ist es nicht die finale Felderkennungsmarke,verliebt zu sein, dass alles nun anders ist, selbst die Dinge, die überhaupt nicht anders sind?

Ich schäme mich, die ganze Zeit du zu sagen. Einige Leute schämen sich, ich zu sagen, ich ich ich, aber ich schäme mich für du dies und du das und du jenes, und immer du und dein in die Sätze zu stecken, die mit mir beginnen. Was ich fühle oder wünsche. Was kann eine Strasse überhaupt wissen? Sie geht, bis sie ankommt, und weiss nicht mal genug, um zu schlafen. Aber was, wenn sie wüsste? Wenn die Strasse wie ein Tempelritter wäre, der gefallen ist, der sich ausstreckt in einem langen Traum vom Sterben, und Männer und Frauen und Ochsen und Schafe würden über seinen Körper hin von Istanbul nach Cadiz ziehen, was würde sein Traum sein? Was wird er uns erzählen, wenn er aufwacht? Seine Hand zerdrückt einen halb gegessenen Pfirsich, saftig, doch ist Staub auf der nassen Frucht. Er empfiehlt Feuchtigkeit, doch er hat Angst zu essen. Weck ihn. Es ist dumm, einfach der Strasse entlang zu gehen. Das ist es, was wir tun müssen. Die Strasse wecken. Und wenn sie aufwacht, wie wird sie sich schämen! Schlafen in der Öffentlichkeit, den Rücken in die Luft und Leute darauf, ihre Finger klebrig und ihr Kopf in

Shame knows him, and he closes his eyes against the accusing sunlight. The sun rises these days like a prosecutor making his last overwhelming speech to the jury before they condemn me to death.

B: *I am ashamed that I'm so crazily touchable, out of control, touch me.*

R: Because you say this, the unicorns of Eden rouse from their sleep, the lost tribes shuffle in from the desert, and the new Temple built exclusively from jewels—the twelve gems of the only genuine signs—rears itself spontaneously from the drowned meadow. Its walls and turrets cast real shadows, shadows that themselves can be lifted from the ground and broken, crackling like spun sugar, crackling like crème brûlée, like old dry bones in a jackal's disappointed jaws, like sunrise on an ominous day, like a slap on the buttock, like a crackle of distant thunder, like a piece of cheese. Because you say this, Barbarossa's elbows slip off the stone table, he falls to the ground. The shock wakes him up, and he finds he is a young man again. He forgets all thoughts of rulership and vengeance, he slips out of the cave and goes to the university to learn argument and love. But I am ashamed to tell you about me. Because a woman says *Touch me, I beg,* why then the world changes. And do you know why? The Chinese poet might have known, I don't think he said so, though, do you know why?

The world changes because all the world is, ever, is an

Spanien! Die Scham kennt sie, und sie schliesst ihre Augen gegen das anklagende Sonnenlicht. Die Sonne erhebt sich heutzutage wie ein Staatsanwalt, der seine letzte überwältigende Rede vor den Geschworenen hält, bevor sie mich zum Tode verurteilen.

B: *Ich schäme mich, dass ich so verrückt berührbar bin, ausser Kontrolle, berühr mich.*

R: Weil du das sagst, erheben sich die Einhörner von Eden aus ihrem Schlaf, die verlorenen Stämme schlurfen herein aus der Wüste, und der neue Tempel, der ausschliesslich aus Juwelen gebaut ist, den zwölf Edelsteinen mit den einzig genuinen Zeichen, erhebt sich ganz spontan von selbst aus der überschwemmten Wiese. Seine Wände und Türmchen werfen richtige Schatten, Schatten, die vom Boden genommen werden können und gebrochen, sie krachen wie Zuckergespinst, sie krachen wie crème brûlée, wie alte trockene Knochen im Rachen eines enttäuschten Schakals, wie der Sonnenaufgang an einem verhängnisvollen Tag, wie ein Schlag aufs Hinterteil, wie das Grollen von weit entferntem Donner, wie ein Stück Käse. Weil du das sagst, rutscht Barbarossas Ellbogen vom Steintisch, er fällt auf den Boden. Der Schock weckt ihn auf, und er findet sich wieder als junger Mann. Er vergisst alle Gedanken an Führerschaft und Rache, er schlüpft aus dem Grab und geht zur Universität, um Argumente zu lernen und Liebe. Aber ich schäme mich, von mir zu erzählen. Nur weil eine Frau: «*Touch me, I beg*» sagt, warum sollte sich die Welt deshalb ändern.

answer to our prayers. That which we beg, that the world becomes. World, the word itself is a doubled thing, something rolled up on itself, rolled so that the front and the back of anything press close together. World means scroll means volumen means volva means Volaspo means vulva means whatever that mouth is which kisses, one lip against the other, and then speaks. The world is what desire speaks. So there you said it, or someone speaking with your mouth said Touch me, I beg. And I heard that, in fact it took me months to hear it, because all that time the old world was falling down, brick dust and mortar dust, cornerstone cracks and the skeletons walk out screaming with their dry mouths, skeletons of human sacrifices immured ages ago as forfeits to the evil power, so that the building would stand. Is all power evil? Does every building stand, embodiment of sin, torture, revenge against the wind, refuge from the light? But because of what that woman said—was it you, did you say it?—because of what she said, the world fell down around the ankles of Rome and the damp old socks of Beijing, and a brand new world had to come up, sleek as an igloo, empty as my head, with a crow sitting on top of it saying Ich bin die Fahne, und ich bin die einzige, und ich bin genug.

B: *Touch me, I beg, I am inconsolable.*

R: Is understanding the same as touching? Standing under, I reach up and touch the sky. Whatever your outstretched hands touch is the sky. The skin. Touch me. Is this right, do I

Und weisst du warum? Der chinesische Dichter könnte es gewusst haben, ich glaube allerdings nicht, dass er es sagte, weisst du warum?

Die Welt ändert sich, weil die ganze Welt, immer, eine Antwort ist auf unsere Gebete. Was wir bitten, das wird die Welt sein. Welt, das Wort selbst, ist ein doppeltes Ding, etwas in sich selbst eingerollt, so gerollt, dass Vorderseite und Rückseite von allem nah aufeinander pressen. Welt bedeutet Schriftrolle bedeutet Volumen bedeutet volva bedeutet Volaspo bedeutet Vulva bedeutet was immer der Mund ist, der küsst, eine Lippe gegen die andere, und dann spricht. Die Welt ist, was die Begierde spricht. So hast du es also gesagt, oder jemand hat es mit deinem Mund gesagt: *Touch me, I beg.* Und ich hörte es, eigentlich brauchte ich Monate, um es zu hören, weil in der ganzen Zeit die alte Welt zusammenbrach, Ziegelstaub und Mörtelstaub, Ecksteinbrocken, und die Skelette gingen schreiend raus mit ihren trockenen Mündern, Skelette von menschlichen Opfern, die vor Jahrhunderten als Pfand für die Böse Macht eingemauert wurden, damit das Gebäude stehen bleibt. Ist alle Macht böse? Steht jedes Gebäude, Verkörperung von Sünde, Tortur, Rache, gegen den Wind, Rückzug vom Licht? Aber wegen dem, was diese Frau sagte – warst du das, hast du das gesagt? – wegen dem, was sie sagte, fiel die Welt runter auf die Fussknöchel Roms und die feuchten alten Socken von Bejing, und eine brandneue Welt sollte auferstehen, schnittig wie ein Iglu, leer wie mein Kopf, mit einer Krähe, die oben aufsitzt und sagt: *Ich bin die Fahne, und ich bin die einzige, und ich bin genug.*

understand? *I am the widowed, I can't be consoled*, said Nerval, is that it? Is touching something only hands can do, skin and its company of knights who sally forth and meet their kindred in the dark, and everything falls away except what they feel? Or is touch another thing? Another French poet wrote: *I cherish the broken watch because it tells a different sort of time*. Is that it? Is that touch, the tick tock of time slipping by, I feel it, a breath on the nape of my neck, Genickschuss, the coup de grâce given by elves, cupids, fairies, trolls, kobolds, a gentlest loving ever-changing touch? A breath?

I am too like you. I am ashamed of being so like you. Forgetting myself, I want to throw my arms around you, hold you. What then? Forgetting myself, all there could be then would be you. You in my arms. It could only happen if I forgot myself. But then whose arms are they if I forget myself, if my self is forgotten? They are the arms the world gives us to know us. Know us, not ourselves. No selves, just us. The given knows us. So it is said that the shaman is made of all the shame in the world, all the resentment and humiliation that has ever been, he smells bad, he looks weird, he does what nobody does and goes to terrible countries inside his shadow, inside his shoes, inside your clothes, he sails down your veins. The terrible shaman is made of shame, a shame man. But he has no shame. I am ashamed of having no shame at all.

B: *Berühr mich, bitte ich, ich bin untröstlich.*

R: Ist verstehen dasselbe wie berühren? Ich mich stelle mich unter, fasse hoch und berühre den Himmel. Was immer deine ausgestreckte Hand berührt, ist der Himmel. Die Haut. Berühr mich. Ist das richtig? Verstehe ich? *I am the widowed, I can't be consoled*, sagte Nerval, ist es das? Ist Berühren etwas, was nur Hände tun können, die Haut und ihre Begleitung, die Ritter, die aufbrechen, um welche von ihrer Art im Dunkeln zu treffen, und alles fällt weg, ausser, was sie fühlen? // *Ich wüsste was von den Riten der Ritter der Haut, wenn du die Richtige bist, wirst du es auch wissen und die antreffen, dort, die von deiner Art sind und dich endlich ablösen von dir und aufnehmen lassen von ihnen, die weit mit dir reiten, ins Glück, von dem du so viel weisst und so wenig siehst durch deine Brille im Freien, und wenn nicht, noch nicht, wenn du noch nicht die Richtige bist, obwohl die Einhörner sich aus Eden erhoben wegen deinem Gebet, wirst du noch einiges Blut im Schnee sehen und Menschen lieben, die es darin verlieren, die du liebst, die dich nicht lieben, weil ihr Blut im Schnee verloren ist. Du wirst das lange nicht verstehen, auf das Blut sehen und warten, und vielleicht bleibt das so.* // Oder ist Berühung eine andere Sache? Ein anderer französischer Dichter schrieb: *I cherish the broken watch because it tells a different sort of time.* Ist es das? Ist das Berühren, das Tick Tack der Zeit, die vorbei streicht, ich fühle es, den Atem im Nacken, *Genickschuss*, der coup de grâce, der Gnadenstoss von Elfen verpasst, Kupido, Feen, Trolle, Kobolde, ein zärtlichster ewig verwandelnder touch, Berührung? Ein Atem? // *Sprich nur ein Wort und alles ist gut.*

Ja. Aber nicht für immer. Sprich für immer ein einziges Wort
und alles ist immer gut. Ja. Als sich seine Hand in deinen
Nacken legte, war alles gut, gegen deinen Willen, denn es war ein
Abschied, dein Körper sagte es dir: Es ist alles gut. Als hättest du
in Milch und Honig gebadet, so hast du ausgesehen. Es gibt aber
keine Zeit. Warum bist du dümmer als dein Körper und warum
hängst du trotzdem so an ihm dran, dass er eingesperrt ist in
deinen Geist, der nichts von ihm weiss. Ich habe keine Lust
mehr, das Glück mit Kübeln über dich zu schütten, sagt Gott,
und die Einhörner und die Juwelen und die Türme. Dann sagst
du etwas Schwieriges, sagst du es zu mir? du sagst: Ich bin jetzt,
wie die weisse Birke, fertig mit der Vorbereitung dafür, dass du
mich geniesst, nicht nur Gott, Gott hat mich immer genossen,
ich weiss, ich weiss das sehr, lieber Gott, bitte mach, dass mich
Menschen geniessen, ein Mensch, ich weiss seinen Namen. //

Ich bin allzusehr wie du. Ich schäme mich, so sehr wie du zu
sein. Mich selbst vergessend, will ich meine Arme um dich
legen, dich halten. Was dann? Mich selbst vergessend, alles
was dann sein könnte, wärest du. Du in meinen Armen. Es
könnte nur passieren, wenn ich mich selbst vergässe. Aber
welche Arme sind es dann, wenn ich mich vergesse, wenn ich
selbst vergessen bin? Es sind die Arme, die uns die Welt gab,
um uns zu kennen. Uns, nicht uns selbst. Kein selbst, nur uns.
Das Gegebene kennt uns. So wird gesagt, dass der Schamane
aus aller Scham der Welt gemacht sei, all die Missgunst und
Demütigungen, die es jemals gab, er riecht schlecht, sieht
verwirrend aus, tut, was niemand tut, und geht in
schreckliche Länder hinein in seinen Schatten, in seinen

Schuhen, in seinen Kleidern, er segelt durch deine Venen. Der schreckliche Schamane ist aus Scham gemacht, ein Schammann. Doch er hat keine Scham. Ich schäme mich, überhaupt keine Scham zu haben.

SHAME 9

Yes. It is always skin. Skin is the border. The breathing border of your prison. The reason for your passion. Skin is the place for sin. Skin is necessary for the ego. So sin. It is even necessary to hurt for the ego like to bleed for the skin, to weep for the sky, eggs for the hen. Skin, through which you are, in which you are born, which bounds you round yourself. The sky is not the limit, I sigh. There is so much skin, and therefore so much border, to cross, even in yourself, even round your spine, your liver // your leave-her //, your heart, in the brain. Working skin. You know this stuff. You wrote it. Your skin is my skin. I will write this pop song for you.

Skin chatters. Skin breathes. Skin conducts. Skin decides, absorbs, never forgets. Skin keeps a record, of everything. Skin refuses. Skin is line for line the book you are. Skin betrays you. Skin is a double agent. In the hand of the enemy begins his love for your skin, when he feels it, when he reads you, it's never without love and this love is never without betrayal. I am ashamed of having been so deceived about people. My cheeks flush with strawberry rashes. I squeeze them myself and whatever I get rid of, I welcome joyously.

SCHAM 9

Yes. It is always skin. Skin is the border. The breathing border of your prison. The reason for your passion. Skin is the place for sin. Skin is necessary for the ego. So sin. It is even necessary to hurt for the ego like to bleed for the skin, to weep for the sky, eggs for the hen. Skin, through which you are, in which you are born, which bounds you round yourself. The sky is not the limit, I sigh. There is so much skin, and therefore so much border, to cross, even in yourself, even round your spine, your leaver, your heart, in the brain. Working skin. You know this stuff. You wrote it. Your skin is my skin. I will write this pop song for you.

Haut plappert. Haut atmet. Haut dirigiert. Haut entscheidet, nimmt auf, vergisst nicht. Haut zeichnet auf, alles. Haut schlägt aus. Haut ist Linie für Linie das Buch, das du bist. Haut verrät dich. Haut ist ein Doppelagent. In der Hand des Feindes beginnt dessen Liebe für deine Haut, wenn er sie fühlt, wenn er dich liest, es geht nicht ohne Liebe und diese nicht ohne Verrat. Ich schäme mich, so enttäuscht über Menschen zu sein. Meine Backen werfen Erdbeerblasen. Ich drücke an mir herum und was ich entlasse, begrüsse ich euphorisch.

Skin pockets full of water. Nervous water. Nourishing water. Water and stone. The spinal column around which we turn, the one you spelled out the letters of, spelled away, swims shamelessly through me. Without I. Stretches out. Drops anchor. Seduces me, to try them out as if they were me, so I'm ashamed. *I always try to comfort the person who makes me cry. I cry: Not guilty, but who?*

When something touches me I am ashamed that I drew it to me. That I touched it. I am ashamed to touch something when I don't know whether it wants to be touched by me, ashamed of doing it secretly, or contriving to make it touch me without knowing me. I am ashamed of knowing more of you than is proper. (Or this is a fantasy. Mine.) I am ashamed that I invent you while I'm knowing you, swallow you up in me because I exist only with you, when I eat you, ashamed that I want you take me to yourself.

The cat has your tongue. At the same moment I say to someone: Say meow. Someone other than you and me. Say just exactly meow. Then I read that the cat has your tongue and your words are licking. Milk. I'm not surprised that you're ashamed. I'm surprised that you shame me. I'm ashamed I took away your cat from your tongue and built it into my piece. (It's called Black & Decker = Black-entdecker = Black Inventor.) Somebody says in it: Say meow. Say just exactly meow. Invention is uglier than truth. More embarrassing. Nakeder. Invention stinks of effort. Protein. Self assertion. It should burst. And my cheeks burst too. I

Hauttaschen, gefüllt mit Wasser. Nervösem Wasser. Nährendem Wasser. Wasser und Stein. Die Wirbelsäule, um die wir uns drehen, die du buchstabiert hast, nachbuchstabiert, schwimmt schamlos durch mich. Ohne ich. Räkelt sich. Ankert. Verführt mich, sie auszuprobieren als Ich, also schäme ich mich. I always try to comfort the person who makes me cry. I cry: Not guilty, but who?

Wenn mich etwas berührt, schäme ich mich, dass ich es zu mir heranzog. Dass ich es berührte. Ich schäme mich, etwas zu berühren, von dem ich nicht weiss, ob es von mir berührt werden will, es heimlich zu tun, oder es dazu zu bringen, mich zu berühren, ohne mich zu kennen. Ich schäme mich, mehr von dir zu kennen, als es anständig ist. (Oder Einbildung: meine.) Ich schäme mich, dich zu erfinden, während ich dich kenne, dich mir einzuverleiben, weil ich nur bei dir bin, wenn ich dich esse, und dass ich will, dass du mich zu dir nimmst.

Die Katze hat deine Zunge. Gleichzeitig sag ich zu Jemand: Rede miau. Jemand anders als du und ich. Rede ganz genau miau. Dann lese ich, dass die Katze deine Zunge hat und dein Reden Lecken ist. Milch. Ich wundere mich nicht, dass du dich schämst. Ich wundere mich, dass du mich schämst. Ich schäme mich, dass ich dir deine Katze von der Zunge nahm und in mein Stück einbaute. Es heisst Blackentdecker. Jemand sagt darin: Rede Miau. Rede ganz genau Miau. Schlimmer als Wahrheit ist Erfindung. Peinlicher. Nackter. Erfindung riecht nach Anstrengung. Eiweiss. Selbstbehauptung. Sie soll platzen. Auch meine Backen platzen gleich. Ich bilde mir ein,

imagine that I sensed the cat thing parallel to yours. I am ashamed of the coincidence. Evidently out of loneliness. I believe it anyhow. I am ashamed to be confused in matters of truth. I am ashamed that the wrong note makes me lose the beat. Every one. That I grow only under the best conditions, or else shame. I fail if I am not loved, magnificently. And then I doubt my own ten toes. Whether I'm a frog. Whether Joachim was Mary's father. I fall out of myself. I stand among school children. I cough. Joachim is Jesus's grampa dammit. The janitor understands me. She is a plant, he thinks, and looks up the thing with Joachim. It is right, says one schoolgirl tenderly to me, can it be right, if I am right for one among so many? How do you find me? How shall we water ourselves? But I am a pan. You crack your egg into me. You enjoy it and leave.

I thought I alone knew that, that the road is a living being. You are something like what I am when I eat mushrooms. I don't eat mushrooms. Giant and dwarf by turns, often changing so fast that the giant is a dwarf. Then the road is Gulliver, and I am wandering lost along him, in his armpits, squeezing. Then you inhale me and sneeze me out. Then I come through you into you, inside you. For a moment you were my graveyard, now already you're my airport. I land on your big toe. It is very big. But still the ego is hidden, I say. I invite you to my couch. How can you be on my couch when I'm sitting on your toe. The one on the couch sets the topic. The one on the toe gets bounced up and down and tells stories. Both wind up in slumber.

parallel zu dir das Katzending empfunden zu haben. Ich schäme mich für die Koinzidenz. Aus Einsamkeit wahrscheinlich. Ich glaube es trotzdem. Ich schäme mich, verwirrt zu sein in Wahrheitsdingen. Ich schäme mich, dass mich der Misston aus dem Takt bringt. Jeder. Dass ich nur unter bester Bedingung wachse, sonst Scham. Ich versage, wenn ich nicht geliebt bin, grandios. Ich zweifle dann an meinen zehn Zehen. Ob ich ein Frosch bin. Ob Joachim der Vater von Maria war. Ich falle aus mir heraus. Ich steh unter Schülern. Ich huste. Joachim ist der Opa von Jesus verdammt. Der Hausmeister versteht mich. Sie ist eine Pflanze, denkt er, und schaut das mit Joachim nach. Es ist richtig, sagt eine Schülerin zärtlich zu mir, ist es richtig, wenn ich für eine unter Vielen richtig bin? Wie findet sie mich? Wie giessen wir uns? Aber ich bin eine Pfanne. Du schlägst in mich dein Ei. Geniesst es und gehst.

Ich dachte, ich weiss das allein, dass der Weg ein Wesen ist. Du bist wie etwas, was ich bin, wenn ich Pilze esse. Ich esse keine Pilze. Riese und Zwerg im Wechsel, manchmal so schnell, dass Riese Zwerg ist. Dann ist der Weg Gulliver, auf dem ich mich verirre, in seinen Achseln, zerquetsche. Dann atmest du mich ein und niest mich aus. Dann bin ich durch dich in dich hineingekommen. Kurz warst du mein Friedhof, schon bist du mein Flugplatz. Ich lande auf deinem grossen Zeh. Der ist sehr gross. Das Ego ist trotzdem versteckt, sage ich. Ich bitte dich auf meine Couch. Wie kannst du auf meiner Couch sein, wenn ich auf deinem Zeh sitz. Der auf der Couch gibt die Stichworte. Der auf dem Zeh wird gewippt und erzählt. Beide

R: How can I hear you without penetrating into your space by doing so?

B: *But before I invited you to invade my space, you were in. That is why you chose me to choose you.* In German, that's difficult. In German everything is difficult, except philosophy. Philosophy is always difficult. How can I give, when I am not I, because I extrude myself, because my arms, when they wrap around yours, are not mine. I have forgotten myself. I perish. How can we stand it? Who am I when I am with you, and who am I when I am in you, when you abandon me there and who had you become when you said: We will go on. Did you wet your pants too, you asked at the crossroads, but you were asking about fear, not about love fluids. Who am I, when I'm ashamed that you read me, and who are you then? If I'm not ashamed, would you be me? But I am ashamed.

R: My head rests in Spain. When you sit on my toe even some more. You are the cobold, I am the Golem, you are the sound, I am the breast, you are Gulliver, I am the Travels. Our luggage sits grinning on a star. Stone? I would love to be steady for you. For me too.

B: I am ashamed of the word lust. I am ashamed to be a person who can be approached about lust. I don't enjoy rush. I struggle with it, which I don't enjoy, that's why you don't have fun with me. I am so ashamed of saying you to you, to so many so few you.

geraten in Schlummer.

R: Wie kann ich dich hören, ohne in deinen Raum zu dringen dabei?

B: But before I invited you to invade my space, you were in. That is why you chose me to choose you. Auf Deutsch ist das schwierig. Auf Deutsch ist alles schwierig, ausser Philosophie. Philosophie ist immer schwierig. Wie kann ich geben, wenn ich nicht ich bin dabei, weil ich mich verströme, weil meine Arme, wenn sie sich um deine legen, nicht meine sind. Ich habe mich vergessen. Ich vergehe. Wie halten wir das aus? Wer bin ich, wenn ich bei dir bin, und wer, wenn ich in dir bin, während du mich verlässt dabei, und wer bist du gewesen, als du sagtest: Wir halten durch. Hast du auch Schiss in der Hose, fragst du auf der Kreuzung, du hast nach Angst gefragt, nicht nach Liebesflüssigkeit. Wer bin ich, wenn ich mich schäme, dass du mich liest, und wer bist du dabei? Wenn ich mich nicht schämte, wärest du dann ich? Aber ich schäme mich.

R: Mein Kopf liegt in Spanien. Wenn du auf meinem Zeh sitzt noch mehr. Du bist der Kobold, ich Golem, du Ton, ich Brust, du Gulliver, ich die Reise. Unser Gepäck sitzt grinsend auf einem Stern. Stein? Ich wäre gerne stabil für dich. Auch für mich.

B: Ich schäme mich für das Wort Wollust. Ich schäme mich, wer zu sein, der auf Wollust angesprochen werden kann. Ich geniesse Rausch nicht. Ich kämpfe mit ihm, was ich nicht

R: Stay with you. I have been with you there, in the spot where someone was not with you. I represent the spot. // *I am the ambassador of that place.* // I represent you where someone is not with you. I step into this place and enjoy you there.

B: Somebody is picked up.

J: Book is not enough. If the angels aren't standing right there, it's not the Bible.

R: Three is shame. To feel approached and not be approached. Just watch. To hear them in the dark. To be the product of what they're doing. Stay in between. Lie in the crack. Be the middle. The bridge. The tunnel. Channel. Not be itself. Should not even be there yet still be thrown into the body.

J: The song is called Weird Destiny. I promise you this song. Now there are two of them already. I am ashamed when I promise you something, because I can't answer, not yet, or can't remember. Not with language. This is the weird thing. Not with language. It keeps getting louder and howls. Not with language. Please not with language. Please right now not with language. I'm dying. Whatever is supposed to save me, that's what kills me. How could this happen? The wave rolls over you and you're looking for a word. That was ok for Moses. You are trapped in an egg, from inside you hear knocking on the shell, that destroys your ability to respond.

geniesse, weshalb du keinen Spass mit mir hast. Ich schäme mich, so viel du zu dir zu sagen, zu so vielen so wenig du.

R: Bleib bei dir. Ich bin bei dir gewesen, an der Stelle, wo jemand nicht bei dir war. Ich vertrete die Stelle. Ich vertrete dich, wo jemand nicht bei dir ist. Ich trete auf dieser Stelle und geniesse dich dabei.

B: Jemand wird aufgelesen.

J: Buch ist nicht genug. Wenn die Engel nicht daneben stehen, ist es nicht die Bibel.

R: Drei ist Scham. Sich angesprochen fühlen und nicht angesprochen sein. Zusehen dabei. Es hören im Dunkeln. Das Resultat davon sein. Dazwischen stehen. In der Ritze liegen. Das Mittel sein. Die Brücke. Der Durchgang. Channel. Nicht es selbst sein. Selbst nicht da sein sollen und doch in den Leib geschmissen.

J: Der Song heisst: Bizarre Bestimmung. Ich verspreche dir diesen Song. Jetzt sind es schon zwei. Ich schäme mich, wenn ich dir etwas verspreche, weil ich nicht antworten kann, nicht jetzt, oder mich nicht erinner. Nicht mit Sprache. Dies ist das bizarre. Nicht mit Sprache. Das wird immer lauter und brüllt. Nicht mit Sprache. Nicht mit Sprache bitte. Bitte sofort nicht mit Sprache. Ich sterbe. Was mich retten soll, tötet mich exakt. Wie konnte das passieren? Die Welle rollt auf dich zu und du suchst ein Wort. Für Moses war das richtig. Du bist in ein Ei

To hell with images. You are ashamed of giving too much. Of having surrendered yourself, before anyone could receive you, of giving yourself away, empty, drained of blood, without seeing anyone there, in your craving to give yourself or some other craving. Holding nothing back, you gave yourself away to someone. You stand there without a heart in front of me and I'm supposed to be ashamed that I haven't taken you completely in, with skin and hair.

You're ashamed of not being able to reciprocate. Always to be in debt. To have put me in the wrong. To be too good for me, because I'm always missing you. You're ashamed that you're not good enough, and I miss you even more. I'm ashamed of not being less than I am. Of taking up space and then you disappear beside me, instead of being inside me. I am ashamed that you are not beside me. I'm ashamed that you don't recognize me. I lick where I talk. I feed the world with ducks. I can't stop joking. I can't live without joking. Heaviness kills me. Women in love let the world drink from them. What would I get if I let myself drink my fill of you? If you're a Bible and you touch me, an angel touches me, a burning bush. I am ashamed of being always less cool than hot. With Napoleon, nobody wanted to be in bed with him. Too hot. I don't want to be with you in the oven, said Louise, who didn't love him. Whoever's freezing should be given a coat. Whoever's hot should get a cold shower. I am the Napoleon of love, of the body. I am the dying swan. Pretty soon I'll be a pop song for you. You're afraid to take aim and then miss the target, afraid to love the mark you hit

gesperrt, hörst es von innen an die Schale klopfen, das sprengt dein Vermögen, dich dazu zu verhalten. Zum Teufel mit Bildern. Du schämst dich, zuviel zu geben. Dich übergeben zu haben, bevor wer dich aufnehmen kann, weggegeben zu sein, leer, ausgeblutet, wen nicht gesehen zu haben in deiner Gier, dich zu geben, oder sonst deiner Gier. Du hast dich rückhaltlos in wen hineinverschenkt. Du stehst da ohne Herz vor mir und ich soll mich schämen, dass ich dich nicht komplett aufgenommen habe mit Haut und Haar.

Du schämst dich, nicht zurückgeben zu können. Immer in der Schuld zu sein. Mich in die Schuld gesetzt zu haben. Zu gut zu sein für mich, weil ich dich immer vermisse. Du schämst dich, nicht gut genug zu sein, und noch mehr vermisse ich dich. Ich schäme mich, nicht weniger als ich zu sein. Den Raum einzunehmen und dass du verschwindest neben mir, statt in mir zu sein. Ich schäme mich, dass du nicht neben mir bist. Ich schäme mich, dass du mich nicht erkennst. Ich lecke wo ich spreche. Ich fütter die Welt mit Enten. Ich kann Witze nicht unterlassen. Ich kann ohne Witze nicht leben. Ich sterbe an Schwere. Frauen in Liebe lassen die Welt von sich trinken. Was empfange ich, wenn ich mich an dir satt trink? Wenn du eine Bibel bist und mich berührst, berührt mich ein Engel, ein brennender Busch. Ich schäme mich, immer weniger kalt zu sein als heiss. Zu Napoleon wollte niemand ins Bett. Zu heiss. Ich will nicht zu dir in den Ofen, sagte Louise, die ihn nicht liebte. Wer friert, dem wird ein Mantel gegeben, wer heiss ist, der kriegt kalte Dusche. Ich bin ein Napoleon der Liebe, des Leibes. Ich bin der sterbende

you didn't aim at, the shame of not being able to survive disappointment. You like maximal control in maximal unconsciousness, nothing less. You can't be possessed. I'll count to three. Is it me? Can't I be possessed? Aren't I possessed, since you possess me, you who reject me.

One. I am autonomous. I am proud. I don't need you. I envy myself. I can feel my life. Even when it doesn't feel good, because I'm free of it. It is mine. I am the right one.

Two. I am ashamed. I am not the right one. Is that all? No. There is still someone. Someone for whom I am not the right one. In order not to be the right one for someone, that someone has to be the right one for me. This no one again. This splendid blue nothing. The crown. My beloved. I shoot with equations at sorrows, and am ashamed of it, after all, it's always sorrow that seduces the Logos.

Three. I am ashamed of being ashamed of not being loved. I am especially ashamed not to be loved right. That someone can love me wrong, what a crime that is. Mine. That somebody loves my shame, that this is the solution, and shame is too small an emotion for that, and it is false shame if it is false love. I am false.

I am ashamed to make you believe something, although it is true that you can grasp me better that way, and then I'm not that thing, although I am that. I am ashamed of not answering, I am ashamed that I walk along beside you

Schwan. Ich bin gleich ein Popsong für dich. Du hast Angst, zu zielen und es zu verfehlen, dazu die Scham, das Treffen zu lieben ohne Zielen, Enttäuschung nicht zu überleben. Du liebst maximale Kontrolle in maximaler Bewusstlosigkeit, nicht weniger. Du bist nicht zu haben. Ich zähle bis drei. Bin ich das? Bin ich nicht zu haben? Bin ich nicht zu haben, weil du mich hast, der mich verwirft.

Eins. Ich bin autonom. Ich bin stolz. Ich brauche dich nicht. Ich beneide mich selbst. Ich kann mein Leben fühlen. Auch wenn es sich nicht gut anfühlt, denn ich bin frei davon. Es ist meins. Ich bin die Richtige.

Zwei. Ich schäme mich. Ich bin nicht die Richtige. Ist das alles? Nein. Da ist noch jemand. Jemand, für den ich nicht die Richtige bin. Um für jemand nicht die Richtige zu sein, muss dieser der Richtige sein. Wieder dieser Niemand. Dieses herrliche blaue Nichts. Die Krone. Mein Geliebter. Ich schiesse mit Gleichungen auf Schmerzen und schäme mich dafür, dabei ist es immer der Schmerz, der den Logos verführt.

Drei. Ich schäme mich für die Scham, nicht geliebt zu werden. Ich schäme mich besonders, nicht richtig geliebt zu werden. Dass jemand mich falsch lieben kann, was für ein Verbrechen. Meines. Dass jemand meine Scham liebt, dass dies die Lösung ist, dafür ist schämen zu klein als Gefühl und es ist die falsche Scham, wenn es die falsche Liebe ist. Ich bin falsch.

keeping in step with you, that I don't walk forcefully with you just being there. I am ashamed of sitting alone in a valley, of climbing into the hot baths and looking at all the lovers and also, // *the procession to the summer grazing lands in the Alps* //, to say hello to the shepherd's new dog, I who am a nicely treated animal, I'm allowed to be there because I file a report. A court dog. // *A hope hound.* //

I promise that I will hear you, whatever you say with your hands. Tomorrow I will listen to a stone for you, one they'll lay on my back the way you lay your words.

Vals

Scham 10

Nun bin ich wirklich beschämt, ich sagte Haut, als ich Himmel meinte, ich habe dich verwirrt, ich habe uns beide verwirrt. Ich habe dich mit der Tag- und Nachtgleiche verwirrt. Ich meine die Sonnenwende.

Wusstest du, dass ich zur Tag- und Nachtgleiche geboren wurde? Wie konnte ich dich mit meinem Geburtstag verwirren. Manchmal schäme ich mich, geboren zu sein.

Könnte das der Ärger sein, wirklich? Nicht die Brillen, die wir beide tragen, nicht die wunden Füsse oder unzulänglichen

Ich schäme mich, dir etwas vorzugaukeln, obwohl es stimmt, damit du mich besser fassen kannst, und dann bin ich es nicht, obwohl ich es bin. Ich schäme mich, nicht zu antworten, ich schäme mich, dass ich parallel geh neben dir her, nicht kräftig mit dir mit. Ich schäme mich, allein in einem Tal zu sitzen, in die Therme zu steigen und all die Liebenden zu betrachten und gleich auf die Alm zu fahren, um den neuen Hund des Schäfers zu begrüssen, ich freundlich behandeltes Tier, das da sein darf, weil es Bericht erstattet. Der Hofhund.

Ich verspreche dir, dich zu hören, was du durch die Hände sagst. Ich werde morgen für dich einem Stein zuhören, den sie auf meinen Rücken legen werden wie du deine Worte.

Vals

SHAME 10

I am ashamed now, really ashamed. I said skin when I meant sky, I confused you, I confused us both. I confused you with the equinox, I mean the solstice.

Did you know I was born on the equinox? How could I confuse you with my birthday. Sometimes I'm ashamed of being born.

Could that be the trouble, really? Not the eyeglasses we both wear or the sore feet or the unsatisfactory relatives, not the white wagon hitched to the golf cart, not the fishermen

Verwandten, nicht der weisse Wagen, der an den Golfkarren gekoppelt ist, nicht die Fischer, die ihren Fang wiegen, nicht der traurige Zigarrenrauch, der aus alten Männern strömt auf ihren Veranden, nicht der unangenehme senffarbene Hund, der unter den Azaleen wartet, nicht der Möwendreck an Deck und der knurrende Kapitän, nicht die Wellen, die die Felsen brechen, und die Felsen nicht, die Muschelschalen für die Vögel brechen, die sie dort runter fallen lassen, nichts von all dem, alles davon, ich schäme mich, geboren zu sein.

Schau, als er ihren Rücken liebkosen wollte, hiess das in Wirklichkeit: Der Rücken zeigt nichts von dem, was der Vorderseite passierte, du kannst das Gesicht nicht am Hintern erkennen, er meinte: Lass mich dich da berühren, wo nie Geschichte passiert ist, wo du weich bist, wo jeder weich ist, wo nichts jemals passiert. Verstehst du nicht, sagt er, ich schäme mich für alles, was jemals passiert ist.

Und als er ihre Brüste streicheln wollte, hiess das: Bring mich zurück in den kindlichen Zustand, wo ich mich nur für das Verlangen schäme, Schreien, Pissen und Scheissen, wo ich mich für das Wachen und Schlafen schäme, wo Scham mein Trost und mein Frieden sein kann, fütter mir das Fühlen deiner Brust, meinte er, lass mich nicht aufwachsen, in diesen finstern Ort hinein, wo Nietzsche steht und auf jeden wartet, der den Fehler macht, ein Buch zu lesen oder Bergluft zu atmen oder eine Blume zu pflücken, hier, und da, blauer Enzian, von der Felskante, lass mich nicht dort sein. Ich möchte mich fürs Verlangen schämen, nicht fürs Bekommen.

weighing their catch, not the sad cigar smoke drifting down from old men on their porches, not the disagreeable mustard-colored dog waiting under the azaleas, not the gull shit on deck and the captain snarling, not the waves cracking rock and the rocks cracking mussel shells for birds who drop them there, none of all this, all of this, I am ashamed of being born.

See, when he wanted to caress her back what it really meant was: The back shows nothing of what happened to the front, you can't tell the face from the rear, he meant: Let me touch you where history never happens, where you are soft, where everyone is soft, where nothing ever happens. Don't you understand, he said, I am ashamed of everything that ever happened.

And when he wanted to caress her breasts, it meant: Restore me to the infant condition where I can just be ashamed of wanting and screaming and pissing and shitting, where I can be ashamed of waking and sleeping, where shame can be my comfort and my peace, feed me from the feeling of your breasts, he meant, and don't let me grow up, into that sinister place where Nietzsche stands waiting for everybody who makes the mistake of reading a book or breathing mountain air or picking a flower, there, and there, a blue gentian, from the cliff edge, don't let me be there. I want to be ashamed of wanting, not of getting. I want to be ashamed of doing nothing but lying here ashamed. I don't want to be ashamed of doing things, I don't want to be

Ich möchte mich dafür schämen, nichts zu tun als hier beschämt zu liegen. Ich möchte mich nicht schämen, Dinge zu tun, ich möchte mich nicht für die Welt schämen.

Oder: Ich möchte mich für die Welt schämen, aber nicht für mich. Das ist die normale Haltung, n'est-ce pas? eines Mannes, der die Morgenzeitung liest. Scheisse. Die Welt ist voll mit schlechten Leuten, die schlechte Dinge tun. Jeder ausser mir. Das ist die normale Haltung des Mannes, der Zeitung liest. Deshalb gibt es für ihn eine Zeitung. *Eine Zeitung*, ein Timing, die Zeit. Schlechte Zeiten. Deshalb ist die Zeitung seit dreihundert Jahren voller schlechter Nachrichten jeden Tag, immer schlechte Nachrichten. // *Siehst du immer wieder dieses immer, siehst du?* // Du denkst ein Tag hin und wieder sei unterschiedlich. Aber nein. Niemals. Alle Nachricht ist schlechte Nachricht. Weil die Menschen sich für die Welt schämen wollen und nicht für sich selbst. Wie Nietzsche, deshalb ist er so populär, besonders bei den Jungen, weil Nietzsche sich für seine Mutter schämt und seinen Vater, seine Mutter Mary und seinen Vater Jesus, seinen Opa Joachim und seine Oma Anna, Hannah, die Gnade GOttes. Er schämt sich für GOttes Gnade, das Geld seines Vaters, er schämt sich für die griechische Sprache, aber nicht dafür, dass er sie beherrscht. Er schämt sich für alles, ausser für sich selbst und seine Begierden und seinen Willen, zu singen. *Flamme bin ich*, sagt er berühmterweise, ich bin eine Flamme, und alles, was ich kann, ist brennen, und ich gebe Licht, während ich brenne, und du wirst dich in meinem Licht aalen und wärmen, und wenn ich zu Ende bin, wirst du herausfinden,

ashamed of the world.

Or: I want to be ashamed of the world but not of me. That is the usual attitude, n'est-ce pas, of a man reading the morning paper. Shit shit shit. The world is full of bad people doing bad things. Everybody but me. That is the usual attitude of the man reading the paper. That is why there is a paper for him to read. Eine Zeitung, a timing. A times. Bad times. That is why the paper is full of bad news every day for three hundred years, always bad news. You'd think one day here and there would be different. But no. Never. All news is bad news. Because the man wants to feel ashamed of the world but not about his own self. Just like Nietzsche, that's why Nietzsche is so popular, especially with the young, because Nietzsche is ashamed of his mother and his father, his mother Mary and his father Jesus, his opa Joachim and his oma Anna, Hannah, the grace of G-d. He is ashamed of God's grace, his father's money, he is ashamed of the Greek language but not of his own mastery of it. He is ashamed of everything but himself and his desires and his will to sing. Flamme bin ich, he says famously, I am a flame and all I can do is burn, and I do give light while I burn, and you will bask in my light and warmth, and when I am finished you'll find that I have burned up the whole world. Your world. Not mine. I am ashamed of my world and turn my back on it.

That's why Nietzsche is popular, more than most philosophers. Philosophie ist schwierig, so sagte die Frau,

dass ich die ganze Welt verbrannte. Deine Welt. Nicht meine. Ich schäme mich für meine Welt und dreh ihr den Rücken zu.

Deshalb ist Nietzsche so populär, mehr als die meisten Philosophen. *Philosophie ist schwierig, so sagte die Frau*, und ich höre auf das, was eine Frau sagt. *Philosophie ist gedacht ohne Denken, ist Gedicht ohne dichten. Lied ohne Musik. Ein griechischer Brunnen wovon kein Wasser mehr giesst.* Ich habe ein Dach auf meinem Haus. Ich sollte mich schämen, Sachen über Philosophie zu sagen, ich, der die Sonnenwende nicht von der Tag- und Nachtgleiche unterscheiden kann, ich bin in einer Nachtgleiche geboren worden, hast du das der Art, wie ich palaver, entnommen? *Mis palabras, los conejos de la yerba*, ich sollte mich für Amerika schämen, ich schäme mich für die Hasen auf meinem Rasen. Ein dunkler Fluss mit Namen Hase floss durch die alte deutsche Stadt. Dort ist nichts mehr passiert seit der Zeit von Hermann dem Cherusker, so fühlte ich mich in Frieden. Ich schäme mich für Geschichte.

Ich kann Haut nicht von Himmel unterscheiden. Das ist mein Problem. Als ich fünf Jahre alt war, las ich ein Buch über Sterne. Das war mein erstes Buch. Ich fing an, die speziellen Stellen meiner Haut zu verstehen. Es ist sehr verwirrend. Jung zu sein, ein Junger zu sein, in einem Haus, das Alte machten, und seinen Weg zu finden hin zu seinem eigenen Platz. Den Weg zu finden zur eigenen Haut durch Hitze und Kälte und nass und trocken. Das Efeu die Ziegelwand hochwachsen fühlen, die Wolken über dem Dach segeln sehen und denken: Das Haus fällt. Sich schämen, das zu denken. Ein Opfer der

and I pay attention, I pay attention to what a woman says. Philosophie ist Gedacht ohne Denken, ist Gedicht ohne Dichten, Lied ohne Musik. Ein griechischer Brunnen wovon kein Wasser mehr giesst. I have a roof on my house. I should be ashamed for saying things about philosophy, I who can't tell the solstice from the equinox, I was born in the equalnight, did you suss that from the way I palaver? Mis palabras, los conejos de la yerba, I should be ashamed of America, I am ashamed of the rabbits on my lawn. A dark river called the Hase ran through the old German town. Nothing had happened there since the time of Hermann der Cherusker, so I felt at peace. I am ashamed of history.

I can't tell skin from sky. That is my problem. When I was five years old I had a book about the stars. That was my first book. I began to understand the special places of my skin. It is very confusing. To be young, to be a young one inside a house that old ones have made, and to find one's way to one's own place. To find the way to one's own skin by heat and cold and wet and dry. To feel the ivy growing up the brick wall, to see the cloud sail over the roof and think: The house is falling. To be ashamed of thinking that. To be a victim of parallax. To see that over a house the sky lives, and says the stars.

I thought a book would tell me what they mean, the stars, so I've always been writing it, is it done yet, have the stars the sky spoke come to speak themselves?

Parallaxe sein. Zu sehen, dass über dem Haus der Himmel lebt und die Sterne sagt.

Ich dachte, ein Buch würde mir sagen, was sie bedeuten, die Sterne, so war ich immer dabei, es zu schreiben, ist es damit getan, sind die Sterne, die der Himmel sagte, dazu gekommen, sich selbst zu sagen?

Den Weg zur eigenen Haut finden, und später stell dir vor: Jeder hat Haut. Was ich fühle, muss jeder fühlen. Deshalb kann ich sagen, was mir gefällt. Ich kann sagen, was immer ich will, da jeder Stern im Himmel lebt, lebt jede Seele innen in der Haut.

Und so ging ich ans Grenzland der Haut, *Markgraf von Hautland*, doch das sagt jetzt nichts. Nun schäme ich mich für meine Haut, und du solltest dich auch schämen, weil du Haut hast, und was hat dir die Haut denn jemals Gutes getan, wozu ist sie gut, alles, was sie tut, ist, uns getrennt halten, und alles, was sie tut, ist fühlen, und zu was ist fühlen gut? Du solltest dich fürs Fühlen schämen. Ich schäme mich dafür, etwas zu fühlen. Aber schämen ist fühlen, oder? Ich schäme mich, alles zu fühlen ausser Scham.

Während ich dies denke, sehe ich eine Spottdrossel auf dem Geländer. Eine Spottdrossel ist ein amerikanischer Vogel in der Grösse einer Drossel, er ist weich und grau, von der Farbe einer alten Konföderiertenuniform, er hat einen schwarzen Kopf und ein glänzendes schwarzes Auge, wie Obsidian, als ob

To find the way to one's own skin and later imagine: Everybody has skin. What I feel, everybody must feel. Therefore I can say what I please. I can say whatever I want, since every star lives in the sky, every soul lives inside skin.

And so to the marches of the skin I went, Markgraf von Hautland, but that means nothing now. Now I am ashamed of my skin, and you should be ashamed too, because you have skin, and what good has skin ever done to you, what good is it, all it does is keep us apart, and all it does is feel, and what good is feeling? You should be ashamed of feeling. I am ashamed of feeling anything. But shame is a feeling, isn't it? I am ashamed of feeling anything but shame.

I see a catbird on the railing as I think this. A catbird is an American bird the size of a thrush, he is smooth and grey, color of an old Confederate uniform, he has a black head and a bright black eye, like obsidian, as if his eyes are older than he is, as if his eyes came from some Mexican volcano and still smolder inside, remembering. This catbird I'm looking at is ashamed, like all birds except the vulture. His every movement is furtive, worried, looking in all directions, back, up, down, around, before he takes hold of something there, what is it, seed, seed, another seed, shame, eat, seed, shame. We should all be ashamed of eating. What do we eat after all except other people. I am old with eating.

If we never ate we would not grow old. Never eat anything. When I was a child, Therese Neumann of Konnersreuth ate

seine Augen älter wären als er selbst, als ob seine Augen aus irgendeinem mexikanischen Vulkan kämen und immer noch sich erinnernd glimmten innen. Diese Spottdrossel, die ich ansehe, schämt sich wie alle Vögel, ausser der Geier. Jede ihrer Bewegungen ist verstohlen, besorgt, in alle Richtungen sehend, zurück, hoch, runter, rundherum, bevor sie dort etwas erspäht, was ist es, Samen, Samen, andere Samen, Scham, Essen, Samen, Scham. Wir sollten uns alle schämen, zu essen. Was essen wir nicht alles, alles ausser andere Leute. Essen machte mich alt.

Wenn wir niemals ässen, würden wir nicht alt. Iss niemals etwas. Als ich ein Kind war, ass Therese Neumann von Konnersreuth nur die heilige Hostie jeden Morgen in der Messe und trank sogar niemals Wasser. Doch sie wurde auch alt und starb, sagen sie. Selbst die heilige Hostie war zuviel Essen. Sei ohne Essen, dann sieh. Ich schäme mich, zu essen. Haben die Katholiken noch keine Heilige aus ihr gemacht? Sie haben viel über sie in der Diozöse von Brooklyn gesprochen, als ich ein Kind war, in der Amtszeit von Pius XII, nun höre ich nichts mehr, doch ich kenne keine Katholiken mehr, alle Katholiken schämen sich heute, die Priester tun den Kindern schreckliche Dinge an, berühren ihre Haut, sie sollten sich schämen, ihren Geist zu berühren, ihren kleinen Geist zu berühren mit wüstem Katholizismus und glühenden Apostelbekenntnissen, was ist der Unterschied, sie sollten sich für das schämen, was sie tun und was sie sagen und was sie berühren und was sie zu berühren verweigern. Das einzige, wofür sie sich nicht schämen sollten, ist die weisse heilige

only the sacred host every morning at Mass and never drank even water. But she too grew old and died, they say. Even the sacred host was too much food. Be without eating, then see. I am ashamed of eating. Did the Catholics make her a saint yet? They used to talk about her a lot in the Diocese of Brooklyn when I was a child, in the reign of Pius XII, now I don't hear anything at all, but I don't know any Catholics any more, all the Catholics are ashamed now, the priests do such terrible things to children, touching their skin, they should be ashamed, touching their minds, their little minds with savage catechisms and fierce Apostles' Creed, what is the difference, they should be ashamed of what they say and what they do and what they touch and what they refuse to touch. The only thing they shouldn't be ashamed of is the white sacred host, simple as a pigeon on the grass, easy as an eel in a canal, quick as a dewdrop to melt in the sun, wonderful as a line of an old poem you remember only that one single line from, only that one line, only that white thing that tastes like hardly anything in your mouth, that sustains life, that is food, that feeds you, that kills.

I am ashamed of the other person inside my skin. I'm not sure who she is. Shame is: she am, am she. Rule of letters: They go in any order. That is how they are different from numbers. When you change the order of numbers, you change the meaning absolutely, the only absolute we have. When you change the order of the letters, you begin to understand the meaning of what the first order of the

Hostie, einfach wie eine Taube im Gras, leicht wie ein Aal im Kanal, schnell wie ein Tautropfen, der in der Sonne schmilzt, wunderbar wie die Zeile eines alten Gedichtes, du erinnerst nur noch diese eine einzige Zeile, nur diese eine Zeile, nur dieses weisse Ding, das wie fast nichts schmeckt in deinem Mund, das das Leben erhält, das Nahrung ist, das dich nährt, das tötet.

Ich schäme mich für die andere Person in meiner Haut. Ich bin nicht sicher, wer sie ist. *Shame is: she am, am she.* Scham ist: schau an: sie bin, sei sie. Regel der Buchstaben: Sie gehen in jede Reihenfolge und sind so anders als Zahlen. Wenn du die Reihenfolge der Zahlen änderst, änderst du die Bedeutung absolut, das einzige Absolute, das wir haben. Wenn du die Reihenfolge der Buchstaben änderst, beginnst du die Bedeutung davon zu verstehen, was die erste Reihenfolge der Buchstaben bedeutete. Scham ist, eine Frau zu sein in mir selbst, wie beschämend, ein anderes Geschlecht zu sein, mit all dem Schmerz, den das erste Geschlecht kennt, verursacht und fühlt, warum ein zweites haben. Doch da ist es, das ist: sie bin: schau an.

Wenn sich einmal die Reihenfolge der Buchstaben ändert, ändert sich alles. Bedeutet das, keine Bedeutung zu haben? Oder alle Bedeutungen? Der alte Priester nannte mich einen Nihilisten, ich verstand ihn nie, ich glaube an alles. Als alter Mann stand er vor der Ikonostasis, zweifelte Gott an, doch nicht die Anbetung. Wer weiss was Gott ist, aber wir wissen, was Anbetung tut. Oder wir sind es, die anbeten. Ich verstand

letters meant. Shame is to be a woman in myself, how shameful, to be another gender, with all the pain the first gender knows and causes and feels, why have a second. But there it is, there she am.

Once the order of letters begins to change, everything changes. Is that what it means to have no meaning? Or all meanings? The old priest called me a nihilist, I never understood him, I believe in everything. He stood as an old man in front of the iconostasis, doubting god but not doubting worship. Who knows what god is, but we know what worship does. Or we are who do worship. I understood him a little, I think he meant I am a nihilist because I believe in all the gods, not just his. As if the strict meaning of everything is nothing.

Is there a philosophy where that is true? I am ashamed of philosophy, that lesbian thing. I am ashamed of being a lesbian, but you must be too, since shame is she in your am too, so there must be two of you, or is there only one of me? I am ashamed of being so infrequent, absent without excuse, sick without remedy, happy without cause, sated without eating, drunk without wine. I am ashamed of my rushes and my Rausch, all I am is Rausch, another woman said that, she was one of my internal lesbians at last, a Yankee woman, a sea woman, a married woman, a far away woman, a dead woman for all I know. Who am I to decide who is alive, am I god? I don't know who is alive and who is dead. Like Rilke's angels, but not otherwise. I am ashamed

ihn etwas, ich glaube, er dachte, ich sei ein Nihilist, weil ich an alle Götter glaubte, nicht nur an seinen. Als ob die strenge Bedeutung von Alles Nichts ist.

Gibt es eine Philosophie, in der das wahr ist? Ich schäme mich für Philosophie, das lesbische Ding. Ich schäme mich, eine Lesbe zu sein, doch das musst du auch, da sie in deinem Sein auch Scham ist, // *Du bist sie: Scham, und du hast sie: Scham, und wenn du nicht nur die Reihenfolge der Buchstaben änderst, sondern auch mal verdoppelst, dann hasst du sie, die Scham, die du bist, und bist einmal doppelt und zweimal in dir selbst gegeneinandergestellt, was du bist und was du hast und hasst, so denk dran, sei weniger, weniger Scham, weniger Haben und Hassen, schau auf den Fluss Hase schamschamschamscham schamschamschamscham schamschamschamscham schamschamschamschamschamschamschamschamschamscham (Bitte singen, auf Betonung dabei achten)* //, also muss es zwei von dir geben, oder gibt es nur einen von mir? Ich schäme mich dafür, so selten da zu sein, abwesend ohne Entschuldigung, krank ohne Heilmittel, glücklich ohne Grund, satt ohne Essen, betrunken ohne Wein, ich schäme mich für meine Räusche und meinen *Rausch*, alles, was ich bin, ist *Rausch*, eine andere Frau sagte das, sie war eine meiner letzten inneren Lesben, eine Yankeefrau, eine Meerfrau, eine verheiratete Frau, eine weit entfernte Frau, eine tote Frau, soviel ich weiss. Wer bin ich, zu entscheiden wer lebt, bin ich Gott? Ich weiss nicht, wer lebt und wer tot ist. Wie Rilkes Engel, aber nicht anders. Ich schäme mich, Engel so sehr zu lieben, ich schäme mich, dass du mich so säuberlich

of liking angels so much. I am ashamed that you figured me out so neatly: You are Rausch, you said, rush and intoxication and raving. I don't need wine, I don't drink wine, I drink only tea and water trying to sober up for forty years, what can I do, I am ashamed to be so known, so exposed, I am ashamed of being Noah, always drunk, always naked, always fondling his daughters, I have no daughters, I am ashamed of having no child.

What if this all were true? What if the shame I confess to is the real shame I feel, or the shame that shapes me?

Shame shapes. It had been raining hard then it cleared, the mist lifted and we could see the far end of the island and the headland of the next island soft and Japanese in fog. Now the fog comes down again and that island vanishes, the end of this island is vague now, like a ghost battleship drifting through Baltic mist. I am ashamed of what I almost said, or did I say it. Maybe it's really me speaking when I say I. Maybe I am really ashamed of what I say I'm ashamed of. I always think that when I say I'm ashamed of something it's really something else I'm ashamed of really. How can I know? Am I god, to know such things? I am ashamed of not knowing such things. I am ashamed of wanting to know them.

You made a very good point. You said: "You can't fulfill your own conditions." You said: "You should be ashamed." But then you took those words away. Maybe away is the way. But

herausgefunden hast: Du bist *Rausch*, sagtest du, Rausch und Trunkenheit und Raserei. Ich brauche keinen Wein, ich trinke keinen Wein, ich trinke nur Tee und Wasser, um seit vierzig Jahren auszunüchtern, was soll ich tun, ich schäme mich, so bekannt zu sein, so ausgestellt, ich schäme mich, Noah zu sein, immer betrunken, immer nackt, immer an seinen Töchtern rummachen, ich habe keine Töchter, ich schäme mich, kein Kind zu haben.

Was, wenn das alles wahr wäre? Was, wenn die Scham, zu der ich mich bekenne, die Scham wäre, die ich fühle, oder die Scham, die mich formt?

Scham formt. Es hatte stark geregnet, dann klärte es sich auf, der Nebel hob sich und wir konnten das entfernte Ende der Insel sehen und die weiche Landzunge der nächsten Insel und Japan im Nebel. Nun kommt der Nebel wieder runter und die Insel verschwindet, das Ende dieser Insel ist undeutlich, wie ein Geisterschlachtschiff, das durch den baltischen Nebel driftet. Ich schäme mich für was ich fast sagte, oder sagte ich es. Vielleicht spreche wirklich ich, wenn ich ich sage. Vielleicht schäme ich mich wirklich für das, von dem ich sage, dass ich mich dafür schäme. Ich denke immer, wenn ich sage, dass ich mich für etwas schäme, dass ich mich für etwas anderes schäme in Wirklichkeit. Wie kann ich's wissen? Bin ich Gott, so was zu wissen? Ich schäme mich, so was nicht zu wissen. Ich schäme mich, so was wissen zu wollen.

Du hast ins Schwarze getroffen. Du sagtest: «Du kannst deine

you were right, I should be ashamed. And so should you, any you. Maybe that is the way. I'll tell you what you should be ashamed of. Then we'll know something. For Christ's sakes, this has to be science, doesn't it? What else is worthwhile? This has to be a serious study of shame, yes? I'll tell you what you should be ashamed of, one by one, all the things, I'll stand at the mirror and gesture and point and mime and mimic, and you stand over there, on the other side of this schmutzy glass I'm writing on, and you'll see what you should be ashamed of. Is that a deal? Topp! said Mephistopheles. But he walked through the world without a mirror. Only a devil can do that.

Here is my mirror. You should be ashamed of not being me. Now we can start to blame each other. How can you love without blame? How can you even care without feeling the virtue of difference, the vices of otherness? Can I be god? How dare you try to be me? How could I be you, when I'm not even me? I am she, it says, this word. If only I could be me. I am ashamed of being I and not being me. What are you really ashamed of? I am ashamed of Wollust because it means to be pleasure in being well and pleasure in willing and pleasure in working your will on the world. Wollust is like Art, it has no opposite. One day I sat for hours trying to think of what the opposite of Art is, its antonym, Gegenteil der Kunst, and I couldn't think of one. I am not ashamed of art, I am not ashamed of pleasure. What is wrong with Wollust? You should be ashamed of being ashamed of Wollust. Wollust is sort of desire sort of lust sort of greed

123

eigenen Bedingungen nicht erfüllen». Du sagtest: «Du solltest
dich schämen». Aber dann hast du diese Worte
weggenommen. Vielleicht ist weg der Weg. Aber du hattest
Recht, ich sollte mich schämen. Und du auch, jedes du.
Vielleicht ist das der Weg. Ich sag dir, für was du dich schämen
solltest. Dann wissen wir was. Um Himmelswillen, das muss
Wissenschaft sein, nein? Was ist sonst was wert? Das muss
eine seriöse Studie der Scham sein, ja? Ich sag dir, für was du
dich schämen solltest, eins nach dem anderen, all die Sachen,
ich stehe vor dem Spiegel und gestikuliere und zeige und
mime und Mimik, und du stehst da drüben, auf der anderen
Seite von diesem schmutzigen Glas, auf das ich schreibe, und
du wirst schon sehen, für was du dich schämen solltest. Ist das
ein Deal? Top, sagte Mephistopheles. Aber er ging ohne
Spiegel durch die Welt. Das kann nur ein Teufel tun.

Hier ist mein Spiegel. Du solltest dich schämen, nicht ich zu
sein. Nun können wir uns gegenseitig Vorwürfe machen. Wie
kannst du ohne Vorwurf lieben? Wie kann dich überhaupt
etwas kümmern, ohne den Vorzug der Differenz zu fühlen,
die Unart der Andersartigkeit? Kann ich Gott sein? Wie
kannst du es wagen, ich zu sein? Wie könnte ich du sein, wenn
ich nicht mal ich bin. *I am she*, sagt es, das Wort, shame, wenn
ich nur mich sein könnte. Ich schäme mich, ich zu sein und
nicht mich. Wofür schämst du dich wirklich? Ich schäme
mich für *Wollust*, weil es Freude ist, wenn es dir gut geht, reine
Freude beim Wollen, beim Arbeiten, der Welt deinen Willen
aufdrücken. *Wollust* ist wie Kunst, sie hat kein Gegenteil. Eines
Tages sass ich da und versuchte, das *Gegenteil von Kunst* zu

sort of happiness sort of wanting sort of angry sort of needing sort of touching. No, Wollust is not touching. Wollust overwhelms without touching. Maybe that is why you're ashamed of it.

But I don't know what you're ashamed of, even now. I stand in front of the glass and I don't see anything you should be ashamed of. Maybe you should be ashamed of me, of talking with me, me being who I am, someone ashamed of being. Maybe you should be ashamed of talking with someone who is ashamed of being. I stand in front of the mirror and see forms pass in and out of me, women come and slip inside me, men arrive and follow them, men and women, and beasts come too and sink through the separation we call skin, painlessly into the interior. I am ashamed of all these people coming into me, and none of them go out. That is the problem: easy in, never out. They sink into me and have no way out, except maybe what I say. Anytime I say anything, it is someone escaping.

Shame is also a garden. This is what I think: There are some monks. They are a small order of monks, they exist in only one small monastery somewhere in the heart of the country. Maybe even they aren't Christian. I don't know what kind of god they have. Do you have a god? I don't even know what kind of god I have. I say: oh god. I say: god damn it. I say: god knows. I say: god bless you. I say: god help us. I say: god be with you, which in English is pronounced good-bye. But I don't know what I'm talking

denken, sein Antonym, Gegenteil der Kunst, und konnte an keins denken. Ich schäme mich nicht für Kunst, ich schäme mich nicht für Freude. Was ist falsch mit *Wollust*? Du solltest dich schämen, dich für *Wollust* zu schämen. *Wollust* ist eine Art Begierde, Art Lust, Art Gier, Art Glück, Art Wünschen, Art wütend, Art Brauchen, Art Berühren. Nein, *Wollust* ist nicht Berühren. *Wollust* überwältigt ohne Berühren. Vielleicht schämst du dich deshalb dafür.

Doch ich weiss nicht, für was du dich schämst, selbst jetzt. Ich stehe vor dem Glas und sehe nichts, für was du dich schämen solltest. Vielleicht solltest du dich für mich schämen, mit mir zu reden, mit mir, der ich der bin, der ich bin, jemand, der sich schämt zu sein. Vielleicht solltest du dich dafür schämen, mit jemand zu reden, der sich schämt zu sein. Ich stehe vor dem Spiegel und sehe Formen, die in mich ein- und austreten, Frauen kommen und schlüpfen in mich hinein, Männer kommen und folgen ihnen, Männer und Frauen, und Tiere kommen auch und sinken schmerzlos durch die Trennung, die wir Haut nennen, ins Innere. Ich schäme mich für alle diese Leute, die in mich kommen, und niemand von ihnen kommt raus. Das ist das Problem: Leicht rein, niemals raus. Sie sinken in mich ein und haben keinen Weg raus, ausser vielleicht durch was ich sage. Jedesmal, wenn ich etwas sage, entkommt jemand.

Scham ist auch ein Garten. Das ist es, was ich denke: Da sind einige Mönche. Da ist ein kleiner Orden von Mönchen, es gibt sie nur in einem kleinen Kloster irgendwo im Herzen des

about. I think of god. I think god is close, close. I think god knows. I think god is irreducible, undemonstrable, unappeasable, undemanding. I think god is presence. But I don't know. I think god is someone walking up the block right now, a girl on a hill, a boy crying under an apple tree. I think the famous sparrow that can't fall from the sky without god seeing it fall is itself god. But I don't know. What do you know? What do you really know?

I am ashamed of knowing so little. Really little. Not even all the words of my own language, let alone yours or anybody else's. Let alone god's language. I think god must be the same as language, what else can know so much or say so much?

But these monks. They have banded together and stay together to know something. And what they have spent their lives knowing is a small patch of ground: thirty meters by thirty meters. They have looped a string all around it, from corner to corner, to mark out visually the boundary of their ground. They call this ground The World. I have told this story before but I can't stop telling it, I am ashamed of being obsessed. They call this ground The World, and they exist to examine and understand it. What they do is simply watch.

Watch and count and name and leave alone. They leave the land alone and see what happens. They say: this is what the world does by itself, we do not interfere, we watch. Plants

Landes. Vielleicht sind nicht mal sie Christen. Ich weiss nicht, welche Art von Gott sie haben. Hast du einen Gott? Ich weiss nicht mal, was für eine Art von Gott ich habe. Ich sage: Oh Gott. Ich sage: Gottverdammtnochmal. Ich sage: Gott weiss. Ich sage: Gott segne dich. Ich sage: Gott hilf uns. Ich sage: Gott mit dir, was Englisch ausgesprochen: *good-bye* ist. Aber ich weiss nicht, wovon ich rede. Ich denke an Gott. Ich denke, Gott ist nah, nah. Ich denke, Gott weiss. Ich denke, Gott ist nicht reduzierbar, unvorzeigbar, unersättlich, anspruchslos. Ich denke, Gott ist Anwesenheit. Doch ich weiss nicht. Ich denke, Gott ist jemand, der gerade den Block runter geht, ein Mädchen auf einem Hügel, ein Junge, der unter einem Apfelbaum weint. Ich glaube, der berühmte Spatz, der nicht vom Himmel fallen kann, ohne dass Gott ihn dabei sieht, ist selber Gott. Doch ich weiss nicht. Was weisst du? Was weisst du wirklich?

Ich schäme mich, so wenig zu wissen. Wirklich wenig. Nicht mal alle Worte meiner eigenen Sprache, ganz zu schweigen von deiner oder von der von irgend jemand anderem. // *Lass deine allein, oder die von irgend jemand anderem.* // Ganz zu schweigen von der Sprache Gottes. Ich denke, Gott muss dasselbe wie Sprache sein, was sonst kann so viel wissen oder sagen?

Aber diese Mönche. Sie haben sich zusammen getan und bleiben zusammen, um etwas zu wissen. Sie weihten ihr Leben der Erforschung von diesem kleinen Fleck Erde: dreissig Meter mal dreissig Meter. Sie haben einen Bindfaden

grow and wither, animals come and go, seasons vary, weather strikes, slowly slowly the population changes, everything changes, and the monks watch.

They are reverent, attentive, thoughtful, never distracted. Just like lovers. But they don't realize the critical mistake they are making every day. Not the Heisenberg problem, not the notion (true in quantum land perhaps less true auf deutschem Boden) that observation affects the process observed. Not that. Their mistake is in taking themselves out of the equation morally, as seeing themselves as unchanging valid cognizers of a changing unself-aware system. But they change. And the system they—with little bits of string, for Christ's sake!—marked out may have a self-awareness of its own. For all we know, that looping of the white string—annually renewed, by the way, as a spring festival, complete with fasting, chanting, processions— actually woke up the ground, woke the land to consciousness. How do we know. One of the monks, Frater Nescio, in fact, began to speculate along these lines many years ago, and was silenced by the Prior of those days. He went on doubting, but said nothing, and continued to take his turn at the observation posts, continued to write down the sedulous, unwearied account of leaf and flower, twig and caterpillar, bird and lizard. He consoled himself with the thought that his writing, his counting, these too were part of the system. In fact, he came to believe shortly before his death, only last winter, that he and the other monks were all the while a part of their land, that they themselves

um ihn herum gespannt, von Ecke zu Ecke, um die Grenze ihres Grundes sichtbar zu markieren. Sie nennen diesen Grund Die Welt. Ich habe diese Geschichte schon einmal erzählt, kann aber nicht aufhören, sie zu erzählen, ich schäme mich, besessen zu sein. Sie nennen diesen Grund Die Welt, und sie existieren, um ihn zu untersuchen und zu verstehen. Was sie tun, ist einfach beobachten.

Beobachten und zählen und nennen und allein lassen. Sie lassen das Land allein und sehen, was passiert. Sie sagen: Das ist, was die Welt von selber tut, wir mischen uns nicht ein, wir beobachten. Pflanzen wachsen und verblühen, Tiere kommen und gehen, Jahreszeiten schwanken, das Wetter schlägt zu, langsam langsam ändert sich die Population, alles ändert sich, und die Mönche beobachten.

Sie sind ehrfürchtig, aufmerksam, fürsorglich, niemals abgelenkt. Genau wie Liebende. Aber sie bemerken nicht den entscheidenden Fehler, den sie jeden Tag machen. Nicht das Heisenbergproblem, nicht die Vorstellung (im Quantenland zutreffend, vielleicht weniger zutreffend *auf deutschem Boden*), dass die Beobachtung den beobachteten Prozess beeinflusst. Nicht das. Ihr Fehler ist es, sich selbst herauszuhalten aus der moralischen Gleichung, sich selbst als unveränderbar, zuverlässige Beobachter eines sich verändernden, sich selbst unbewussten Systems zu sehen. Doch sie verändern sich. Und das System, das sie, um Gotteswillen! mit kleinen Stücken Bindfäden markierten, könnte ein Bewusstsein von sich selbst haben. Nach allem,

were the self-awareness of the system.

How absurd they are, these monks I am. Yet they know something about the world. They know the difference between Crassula oponaciformis and a shamrock, they know the things I don't know, the monks I am are rich with knowledge I don't have. These monks of mine are like the human race, and me like a well-known God, he made them, but he doesn't know what they're talking about, he doesn't know the subtle distinctions of sensibility, art history, the avant-garde. I tell you of the monks, I tell you what they know. And I don't know.

I should be ashamed of knowing so little.

was wir wissen, hat dieses Spannen des weissen Bindfadens – jährlich erneuert übrigens als Frühlingsfest, komplett mit Fasten, Singen, Prozessionen – den Boden geweckt, das Land ins Bewusstsein geweckt. Woher sollen wir das wissen. Einer der Mönche, Pater Nescio, hat tatsächlich vor langen Jahren begonnen, diesen Bindfädenzeilen entlang zu spekulieren, und wurde durch den Prior seinerzeit zum Schweigen gebracht. Er zweifelte weiter, sagte aber nichts und nahm auch weiter seinen Beobachtungsposten ein und fuhr fort, die eifrigen und unermüdlichen Aufzählungen von Blättern und Blumen, Zweigen und Raupen, Vögeln und Eidechsen aufzuschreiben. Er tröstete sich mit dem Gedanken, dass sein Schreiben und sein Zählen auch Teil des Systems seien. Kurz vor seinem Tod, erst letzten Winter, kam er zu der Überzeugung, dass er und die anderen Mönche die ganze Zeit Teil ihres Landes waren und sie selbst die Selbstwahrnehmung des Systems.

Wie absurd sie sind, diese Mönche bin ich. Aber sie wissen etwas über die Welt. Sie wissen den Unterschied zwischen Crassula oponaciformis und einem Feldklee, sie wissen Dinge, die ich nicht weiss, die Mönche, die ich bin, sind reich an Wissen, das ich nicht habe. Diese meine Mönche sind wie die menschliche Gattung, und mir wie ein bekannter Gott, er machte sie, aber er weiss nicht, über was sie reden, er weiss nichts von den subtilen Unterschieden von Empfindsamkeit, Kunstgeschichte, der Avantgarde. Ich sag dir was von den Mönchen, ich sag dir, was sie wissen. Und ich weiss nicht.

Ich sollte mich schämen, so wenig zu wissen.

SHAME 11

His river is a hare, he can't tell to flee from to flow. He can't tell his house from his history and even not from his body, and inside himself his wife in him can't tell his man from his wife, this may be wavy, like waving the tail under the azaleas, vague, like you can't tell your tail from your talk, but she thinks, these are the few reasons in the world why you should not be ashamed. I too am ashamed of having been born, she says, that she was not taken back, not taken at all. Her fear, she says, is not to be able to die, to have to wander around the universe forever all by herself alone, not even being nourishment for the stars.

I have been much more ashamed of not eating than of eating. Not eating emphasizes eating. Eating alleviates eating. It's good, you say, when we mutually satisfy each other. The way you say My greedy one, I love my greed. As a holy person I ate nothing for a long time and admired my willpower over my body. But my soul took no pleasure in living longer in this will, and temporarily disconnected. A girl next to me for years relieved herself in the cellar because of the food she ate all day long, she was shame. Besides, she wanted to disappear, so her father couldn't see her. Seeing means seizing. Shame is such a secret public thing. Good for witches and borderline creatures // *who fly on their fenceposts to the sabbat* //. The burning cheeks and the soul

His river is a hare, he can't tell to flee from to flow. He can't
tell his house from his history and even not from his body,
and inside himself his wife in him can't tell his man from his
wife, this may be wavy, like waving the tail under the azaleas,
vague, like you can't tell your tail from your talk, but she
thinks, these are the few reasons in the world why you should
not be ashamed. Auch ich schäme mich, geboren zu sein, sagt
sie, dass sie nicht zurückgenommen wurde und auch nicht
angenommen. Ihre Angst, sagt sie, ist die, nicht sterben zu
können, im All mutterseelenallein für immer herumzuirren,
nicht mal Nahrung für Sterne.

Ich habe mich noch viel mehr geschämt, nicht zu essen, als zu
essen. Das nicht Essen betont das Essen. Das Essen erleichtert
das Essen. Es ist gut, sagst du, wenn wir uns gegenseitig stillen.
Wie du meine Gierige sagst, liebe ich meine Gier. Als Heilige
ass ich sehr lange nichts und bewunderte meinen Willen über
meinen Körper. Doch meine Seele hatte keine Lust, weiter in
diesem Willen zu wohnen, und haute vorübergehend ab. Ein
Mädchen neben mir erleichterte sich jahrelang im Keller um
ihr Essen, das sie tagsüber ass, sie war die Scham. Ausserdem
wollte sie verschwinden, damit ihr Vater sie nicht sehen kann.
Sehen heisst Nehmen. Scham ist eine solche geheime
öffentliche Sache. Gut für Hexen und Zaunwesen. Die
brennenden Backen und die in sich selbst verkrümelte Seele,

shrinking into itself, in the stinging jellyfish within, skin streaked with the touch of it and burned. The red skin, streaked by the jellyfish, and the wobbling jellyfish itself, that coils its way searing inside.

Shame is an animal. When everything's ok, it's a damp hedgehog. I have been swallowed by the animal. I am the animal. And you are the animal also. I am ashamed of my greed. For my hunger. *Easy in, never out.* I am ashamed of not having borne you, says a woman to her unborn child. I would not be ashamed of not being born. Inconceivable, that people strive to be close to other people, to touch their skins, to achieve mutual interaction of their mucous membranes.

SCHAM 12

Alles, was ich tu, ist falsch. Es ist oft schön und falsch, oder weise und falsch, oder dumm und falsch, *doch immer falsch. Ich schäme mich immer irgendwo zu sein, irgendwo* überhaupt, irgendwo ausserhalb der Welt *wie Baudelaire hat es bemerkt, und hier springen die Brücken über die Donau wie Feuer das die trockne Roggenfelder zu küssen kommt,* falsch, da ist kein Fluss, keine Soldaten, *die Soldaten sind tot* und *ihre einmal puterrote Blumen jahrhundertlang gewelkt.* Ich las ein Buch, als ich ein Kind war, dachte ich, ich sei eine Person, ich sass also in meinem Zimmer und las ein Buch, die Jungen kamen vorbei und spotteten laut, da ist er, er liest ein Buch. Und sie gingen runter zum *Messegelände und dort könnten sie die Mädchen*

innen in der Feuerqualle, und von ihr gestreift mit der Haut und verbrannt. Die rote, von der Qualle gestreifte Haut und die quabblige Qualle selbst, die dich verzehrend nach Innen schlingt.

Die Scham ist ein Tier. Wenns gut geht ein nasser Igel. Ich bin vom Tier verschlungen. Ich bin das Tier. Und du bist auch das Tier. Ich schäme mich für meine Gier. Für meinen Hunger. Easy in, never out. Ich schäme mich, dich nicht geboren zu haben, sagt eine Frau zu ihrem nichtgeborenen Kind. Ich würde mich nicht schämen, nicht geboren zu sein. Unvorstellbar sind Menschen, die die Nähe anderer Menschen suchen, um die Häute zu berühren, mit den Schleimhäuten in gegenseitigem Austausch zu sein.

SCHAME 12

Everything I do is wrong. It is often beautiful and wrong, or wise and wrong, or stupid and wrong, doch immer falsch. Ich schäme mich immer irgendwo zu sein, irgendwo at all, anywhere out of the world wie Baudelaire hat es bemerkt, und hier springen die Brücken über die Donau wie Feuer das die trockne Roggenfelder zu küssen kommt, wrong, there is no river, no soldiers, die Soldaten sind tot und ihre einmal puterrote Blumen jahrhundertlang gewelkt. I was reading a book, when I was a child I thought I was a person, so I sat in my room reading a book and the boys came by and sneered out loud, there he is, reading a book. And they went down to the Messegelände und dort könnten sie die

berühren, und während ich las, driftete mein Geist ab vom Buch und hinaus in die Septembernacht und ich wollte sie auch berühren, den weissen Satin auf ihren reifen sizilianischen Brüsten, den schwarzen Satin auf ihren übertriebenen Barihüften, nichts war unter den Kleidern, nichts als blosse Form. *Blosses Gestalt. Doch reines auch, wie ein Gedächtnis das ein Mann oder ein Kind in seiner Hand halten darf, bis seine kluge Haut ihre Investigation fertiggemacht habe*, und der Geist schlief um die Form herum, die er fühlte.

Es macht keinen Sinn, irgend jemand berühren zu wollen. Wie ich es geschrieben finde: Was für seltsame Leute Leute sind, dass sie sich gegenseitig aussuchen für einen Austausch der mucus membrane. *Schleimhäute, erlautet der Text.* Doch was schmecken sie, wenn sie ihre Zungen so zutraulich in den feuchten Mund des anderen legen? Er würde sich genauso wohl fühlen, denkt er, wenn sie niemals mehr sprechen würden, jeder Kuss ist ein Goodbye, warum nicht, die Zunge sagt der Zunge die Wahrheit, *lebwohl mein braver Gardeoffizier*, das will er sie sagen hören, adieu, *vieux chanson*. Er würde sich eigentlich genauso wohl fühlen, wenn er sie nie wieder sehen würde, und wenn Wohlfühlen eine Weise wäre, wie man sein könnte, wäre er diese Weise, er würde auf diese Weise sein und so seinen Weg gehen und sich nie mehr mit ihr herumquälen. All ihr *Geschrei*, alle ihre Forderungen. Bitter dachte er an den grossen französischen Arzt, *das Lied ist aus*, wonach der Patient verlangt, ist niemals das, was der Patient wünscht. Lacan sagt, *demande*

Mädchen berühren, and as I was reading my mind drifted away from the book and out into the September night and I wanted to touch them too, the white satin on their ripe Sicilian breasts, the black satin on their exaggerated Bari hips, nothing was under the cloth, nothing but shape itself. Blosses Gestalt. Doch reines auch, wie ein Gedächtnis das ein Mann oder ein Kind in seiner Hand halten darf, bis seine kluge Haut ihre Investigation fertiggemacht habe, and the mind sleeps around the shape of what it felt.

It makes no sense to want to touch anybody. As I find written: what strange people people are, that they seek one another out for a mutual exchange of mucus membrane. Schleimhäute, erlautet der Text. But what do they taste when they lay their tongues so trustingly inside the damp mouth of another? He would be as comfortable, he thinks, if they never spoke again, any kiss is a goodbye, why not, tongue tells tongue the truth, lebwohl mein braver Gardeoffizier, that's what he wants to hear her say, adieu, vieux chanson. He'd be as comfortable if he never saw her again, actually, and if comfort were a way one could be, he would be that way and take that way and never be bothered with her again. All her Geschrei, all her demands. Bitterly he thought about the great French doctor, das Lied ist aus, what the patient asks is never what the patient wants. The demande is never the true désir. What she talks about is never what she means, why not try silence? Silence of the Persian Gulf, yes, he was happy there, the lazy plump girls of Dubai, so bored they'd do anything. He'd be as comfortable

(Verlangen) ist nie wirklich *désir* (Wunsch, Begehren). Worüber sie redet, ist niemals das, was sie meint, warum nicht Schweigen versuchen? Das Schweigen des Persischen Golfs, ja, er war da glücklich, die faulen prallen Mädchen von Dubai, sie waren so gelangweilt, sie würden alles tun. Er würde sich genauso wohl gefühlt haben, wenn er nie wieder etwas von ihr gehört hätte. Doch ist «nie» ein Zustand innerhalb unserer Reichweite? Die Dinge überreden sie zu einem Kontakt miteinander, ihre Schleimhaut würde eine kostbare Flüssigkeit absondern, die ihre wütende Lust in Worte destillierte, oft zart, oft provokativ, *zart, anreizend*, ihre weiche feuchte Zunge würde sie sprechen, seine trockenen Ohren würden sie hören und seine trockenen Hände berühren.

Es war die Weise, wie sie berührt werden wollte, die ihn sie berühren wollen liess. Als ob seine Hände ihre Diener wären, nicht seine eigenen, als ob sie die Oper wäre, die er so tapfer Nacht für Nacht aufzuführen hätte, sich das Herz aus dem Leib singend, alle seine Kraft und Besitztümer in den Dienst der Musik gestellt, die er nicht mal mochte, ihr Schrei, ihre nicht endenden lyrischen Forderungen. Nur ihre Ängste wechselten ab. Nur die Prädikate in ihren endlosen Sätzen. *Sätze. Was ist ein Satz?* Ein Satz ist ein Sagen, eine sentence, ein Gesetz, ein Sprichwort, eine Bewegung eines Geigenquartetts oder Symphonie oder Sonate. Alle ihre Sätze waren die Violine, all sein Schweigen und seine gelegentlichen Bemerkungen waren das Grollen des Pianos, des Begleiters. Ein Mann, der mit einer Frau die Liebe macht, ist ein Begleiter.

if he never heard from her again. But is 'never' a condition within our reach? Things kept talking them into contact with each other, her mucus membrane would ooze a precious liquid that her angry lust would distill into words, often tender, often provocative, zart, anreizend, her soft moist tongue would speak them, his dry ears would hear, and his dry hands would touch her.

It was the way she wanted to be touched that made him want to touch her. As if his hands were her servants not his own, as if she were the opera he had to perform so bravely night after night, singing his heart out, all of his powers and properties put into the service of this music he didn't even like, her cry, her neverending lyric demand. Only her anxieties changed. Only the predicates in her interminable sentences. Sätze. Was ist ein Satz? A Satz is a saying, a sentence, a law, a proverb, a movement of a string quartet or symphony or sonata. All of her sentences were the violin, all of his silences and occasional remarks were the rumble of the piano, the accompanist. A man who makes love to a woman is an accompanist.

He stood on the beach looking at the surf arriving, die Brandung, interminable waves of her sentences, her needs, her anxieties, her desires, he never wants to hear from her again, but never is so hard, it is the way she wants him to touch her that makes him want to touch her, this same way makes never shorter, never lasts only an hour or a day, then things speak their story and she is with him again. What has

Er stand am Ufer und schaute den ankommenden Wellen zu, *die Brandung*, unendliche Wellen ihrer Sätze, ihrer Bedürfnisse, ihrer Ängste, ihrer Begierden, er wollte nie wieder von ihr hören, doch nie ist so hart, die Weise, wie sie möchte, dass er sie berührt, macht, dass er sie berühren möchte, und das nie kürzer, nie dauert nur eine Stunde oder einen Tag, dann erzählen die Dinge ihre Geschichten, und sie ist wieder mit ihm zusammen. Was hat sein Wille damit zu tun? Der Wille ist das Gegenteil von Lust. Wissen die Philosophen das? Las er es, oder ist es etwas, eine schmerzliche kleine hölzerne Nadelknotenwahrheit, die er am Ende seines Lebens in seinen Händen fand? Das Leben endet immer. Er muss sie verlassen, er muss sie jetzt verlassen. *Brandung* klingt mehr nach Feuer als nach Wasser, die Brandung in ihrem weichen kleinen Mund kann ihn verbrennen, die Dinge, die sie sich gegenseitig antun mit ihren plötzlichen flattrigen Forderungen. Er muss sie auf ihrem Balkon lassen, in ihrem Appartment in Genf lassen, in ihrer Villa in der Toskana, in ihrer Hütte auf Teneriffa, ihrem Haus in den Hügeln über Corinth, egal welche Sprache sie jetzt durch ihre Schleimhäute auf ihn spuckt, es muss Goodbye für ihn sein. Ihr dummer Balkon. Ihre dummen Tränen. Eine Frau sollte stolz sein, wenn ein Mann sie verlässt, es bedeutet, sie ist zu stark für ihn, er gibt es zu, er läuft weg. Es ist da keine andere Frau ausser der Welt. Es ist da keine andere Frau ausser Schweigen. Es ist da keine andere Frau ausser ein Lied von Debussy oder ein Poster von Dominique Sanda, bereit, sich zu töten, alle Frauen sind Selbstmörderinnen, alle Männer sind Mörder, da ist kein anderer Ausweg aus diesem Dilemma. Ein

his will got to do with it? The will is the opposite of lust. Do philosophers know that? Did he read it, or is it something, a painful little wooden pine-knot truth-like thing he has found in his hands at the end of his life? Life is always ending. He has to leave her, and leave her now. Brandung sounds more like fire than like water, the surf inside her soft small mouth can burn him, the things they do to each other with their sudden fleeting demands. He has to leave her on her balcony, leave her in her apartment in Geneva, leave her in her villa in Tuscany, her cabin on Teneriffe, her house in the hills above Corinth, no matter what language she gets her mucus membrane to spit out to him now, it must be goodbye for him. Her stupid balcony. Her stupid tears. A woman should be proud when a man leaves her, it means she is too strong for him, he admits it, he is running away. There is no other woman but the world. There is no other woman but silence. There is no other woman but some song by Debussy or a poster of Dominique Sanda ready to kill herself, all women are suicides, all men are murderers, there is no other way out of this predicament. A pre-dica-ment is a Satz formed before it is spoken, a thing a god made but there is no god. Bon soir, beau soir, beautiful night that takes the sight of her away, he thinks, but leaves the feeling of her hips in his hands.

Steissbein. Schlüsselbein, end to end of the torso, the Dogon say the clavicle is the oldest of all things, the world was made from a collarbone, but whose? From the collarbone hangs the curtain of the Temple, this pink veil

pre-dica-ment ist ein Satz, geformt, bevor er gesprochen ist, etwas, was Gott gemacht hat, aber es gibt keinen Gott. *Bon soir, beau soir,* schöne Nacht, denkt er, die ihren Anblick wegnimmt, doch das Gefühl ihrer Hüften in seinen Händen lässt.

Steissbein. Schlüsselbein, Anfang und Ende vom Torso, die Dogon sagen, das Schlüsselbein sei das älteste von allen Dingen, die Welt wurde aus einem Schlüsselbein gemacht, doch wessen? Vom Schlüsselbein hängt der Vorhang des Tempels, dieser rosa Schleier runter, nass von unserem Schleim. Nein, erklären sie, der Knochen kam zuerst, niemand war vor dem Knochen, es war niemands Knochen, *Niemandsbein,* nicht in Schweden, nicht in Afrika, nicht in Australien, wo die Götter keine Münder haben.

Und wie suchen die Träume die Knochen dieser anderen Frau heim? Wie schlägt er sie, der Traum, quetscht die Haut um den Steiss, vergiss nicht die Peitsche, wenn du träumen gehst, kriecht der Traum unter uns her und wird Grund, der harte Stein, auf dem wir ausruhen, bis unsere Knochen wund sind.

Die Mysterien. Die Flöte des Trolls, die er neben der See spielen hört, oder unter ihr, kann da unten Musik sein? Grünes Sehen, grünes Sähen, grüne See, sagt sie. Die Trollmusik, die Trollharfe hat Eisensaiten und Lautsprecher aus Lindenholz, *Lindenbaum,* jetzt weiss er, wo er ist. In La Plage de Départs, wo er seinen Abgang erklärt und wieder von ihr Abschied nimmt. Aber er merkt, dass er nur zur See spricht. Ihr grüner

wet with our mucus. No, they explain, the bone came first, there was no one before the bone, it was no one's bone, Niemandsbein, not in Sweden, not in Africa, not in Australia where the gods have no mouths.

And how do dreams afflict that other woman's bones? How does the dream beat her, bruise the skin around the coccyx, don't forget the whip when you go dreaming, is it that the dream creeps beneath us and becomes the ground, the hard stone on which we rest until our bones are sore?

The mysteries. The troll flute he hears playing beside the sea, or under it, can there be music under there? Green seeing, green seeding, green seas she said. The troll music, the troll harp has iron strings and basswood sound box, Lindenbaum, he knows where he is now. It is La Plage de Départs, where he swears his oath of resignation and takes leave of her again. But he finds that he is speaking only to the sea. Its green sound speaks back to him. Das Meer. Neutrum. But he has to hear the woman, we can't let him off the hook, he has to hear her consent to his departure.

I consent to my dismemberment, is what he wants her to say.

Sound antwortet ihm. *Das Meer. Neutrum.* Aber er muss die Frau anhören, wir können ihn nicht von der Angel lassen, er muss ihre Zustimmung zu seiner Abreise hören.

Er möchte, sie sagt, Ich bin einverstanden mit meiner Zerstücklung.

And now to the Stones
PROMISED POP SONG NUMBER ONE

To the mothers we have to travel through the stones, hard
it's hard, the mother, the one I mean, I have to feed
the mother with the stones, I
that she, me, better rather never
not even pigs, Hades
has a swan's neck, no castle down there
hard bread with mold on it they push fat stones down my
                                                        neck

now I am unfoddered, gravel in the mouth from you
you Beckett, Ponge, my father
I lust
for the whole body, lust
the German Angst
is missing
what's left is apricots, stones, soap

Through the breaches which are beaches in the marches
go the bridges through the quarry, through eyes, roses
                                        through oranges,

Und jetzt zu den Steinen
PROMISED POP SONG NUMBER ONE

Zu den Müttern muss ich durch die Steine, hart
ist es, die Mutter, die ich meine, muss ich füttern
ich, die Mutter mit den Steinen
die sie, mir, wie besser lieber niemals
nicht mal Schweinen, Hades
Schwanenhals hat es, kein Schloss
hartes Brot mit Schimmel damals durch den Hals gab sie mir
fette Steine
jetzt bin ich ungefüttert, Kiesel im Mund von dir
du Beckett, Ponge, der Vater
ich Lust
am ganzen Körper, Lust
the German Angst
verpasst
bleiben Aprikose, Steine, Seife

Durch die Brüche geht die Brücke durch den Steinbruch
durch Augen, Rosen durch Orange, press den Pass
Nelken, Beine, die ich meine, fallen Steine

press the pass, carnations, legbone, the one I mean, stones
                                                    fallen

through trousers, upright
legs shrivel
I fall in *through blood and mud to the green feelings*
beyond, death is gain
the German passage again

and all the horses gallop to you
never eat oranges at the full moon: Saburo Teshigawara:
I dance the soul of my neighbor
the earth stammers
the crack opens up and the mother

wants to translate
is hungry
knows no English
so I do the talking

In some cosmic operation
some translation
some somnambulation
station, sweet cooperation
with ghosts
Gespenster
of yesteryear
so fresh, flash me
dead bones

durch Hosen, lotrecht
Beine welken
fall ich ein through blood and mud to the green feelings
beyond, death is gain
the German passage again

Und alle Pferde rasen zu dir
iss niemals Orangen bei Vollmond: Saburo Teshigawara:
ich tanze die Seele meines Nachbarn
die Erde stottert
Spalt öffnet sich und die Mutter

will übersetzen
hat Hunger
versteht kein Englisch
deshalb sprech ich

In some cosmic operation
some translation
some somnambul station
some sweet cooperation
mit Geistern
with ghosts
von gestern
so fresh, flash me
dead bones

He looks like almost beeing born, eyes closed, forehead
closed, mouth wet and laughing in dark despair, filled with

He looks like almost being born, eyes closed, forehead closed,
mouth wet and laughing in dark despair, filled with pills,
filled with all the young murders, the slaughtered mothers, my
new forensic friend from Southend and I, my transparent spy,
incognito, so:

When I cry, some chick sings on the radio
stones in my bed, stones in my eyes
are these extraterrestrial spies
what I know is what she sang, when she got me
I am your mother and you are the stone
I am not happy and you will be born
evil go home

You ergot on my rye bread o my mother
sick with St Anthony's fire, ergot poison,
green as Grünewald
something happens there again
like showing off, cutting, splitting, bashing, sawing
stone is small against water, stone is a lake
a very fluent thing, the mountain itself
knows how to flow, mommy
the rose, the Pentecost tongues of fire, I see you
green like your goat dream goat trance
where I am at home

The brood mare hurries under the earth
it is her sky
the sentence is not out of whack, it is correct, my

pills, filled with all the young murders, the slaughtered
mothers, my new forensic friend from Southend and I, my
transparent spy, incognito, so:

Wenn ich weine, singt im Radio eine
stones in my bed, stones in my eyes
are these extraterrestrial spys
was ich weiss, ist, was sie sang, als sie mich bekam
I am your mother and you are the stone
I am not happy and you will be born
evil go home

Du Mutterkorn, sackheiliges Feuer
der Mutterkornkranken
du Antoniter
etwas geschieht da wieder
wie sprengen, schneiden, spalten, schlagen, sägen
Stein ist gegen Wasser klein, dass er ein See ist
ein sehr flüssig Ding, der Berg, selbst, Mama
die Rose, die Zunge Pfingsten, ich seh dich
grün wie deine Ziegentrance
in der bin ich zuhause

Die Stute eilt unter der Erde
sie ist ihr Himmel
der Satz ist nicht aus den Fugen, er ist in Ordnung, mein
ganzer Stein schrie erlöst

Grün sehen, Steine klopfen, Zeit ansetzen, Möslein sagen auf

whole stone shouted out released

Green seeing, stones beating, time estimating, little cunts, *Möslein auf der Heide*, telling on the heath, run for your life, not one left upright upon another, not even, when love, karma, the sweet, the comatose, Kama Sutra, so many jobs, these acorn oaks, it overflows, the way all pleasure perishes and screams and Eternity expels itself with that dwarf Time, you must concentrate on the staff, he says, not on the egg, that flies away, Indians, kids, arrows in pants pockets, they want to slurp up sugar sweet bunny girls in Cologne, skull fractures, bones, o I forgot, I'm an egg, I'm big, pulsating, of luminous green, before it's there, the flower goes out in the stone.

And now
SHAME 13

Can he tell his horse from his bird. (Can he tell his hers from what hurts.) Can he tell ears from telling. Can he tell her back from his spelling. Can he tell her death (her dad) from his finger, as it's written by her (Sexton): He (Godfather) put a finger on his back / for the big blackout / the big no. So: Can he tell writing from riding and riding from dying (riding the black back).

How can touching ever happen, where nothing ever happens, you say, where they are soft. How can he understand himself under the stars, that up there tell him

der Heide, um das Leben rennen, weil keiner auf dem anderen
bleibt, auch nicht, wenn Liebe, Karma, die Süsse, die
komatöse, Kamasutra, die stellungsreiche, diese Eicheleiche,
die überfliesst, wie alle Lust vergeht und schrie und Ewigkeit
sich mit Zwerg Zeit vertreibt, du musst dich auf den Stab
konzentrieren, sagt er, nicht auf das Ei, das fliegt ab, Indianer,
Jungen, Pfeile in Hosentaschen, wollen in Köln
Mädchenkaninchenjagenvernaschen, Kehlkopfkrachen,
Knochen, ich habs vergeigt, ich Ei, ich gross, pulsierend, von
leuchtendem Grün, ehe es da ist, löst sich die Blume im Stein.

Und jetzt
SCHAM 13

Can he tell his horse from his bird. (Can he tell his hers from
what hurts.) Can he tell ears from telling. Can he tell her back
from his spelling. Can he tell her death (her dad) from his
finger, as it is written by her (Sexton): He (Godfather) put a
finger on his back / for the big blackout / the big no. So: Can
he tell writing from riding and riding from dying (riding the
black back).

Wie kann Berühren da passieren, wo niemals etwas passiert,
sagst du, wo sie zart sind. Wie kann er sich verstehen unter
den Sternen, die ihn da oben – wie in den Sternbüchern im

—as in the star books he looked at in bed—as they tell themselves. How can dying be living, as they say. How can the star know you, and how important is that to you.

I have a new angel: the ape. He appears to me in Vals. I have. I don't have. A monk doesn't think this way. I am no monk, and I shouldn't be ashamed of that. I should be ashamed that I want to be a monk. I really don't want that. The ape from Vals is sly. He tells me something that I never want to forget, after I buried myself in his arms. Of course I knew that I had lost an ape and was supposed to make up one in myself, in which I could sleep. Not for always. An ape as a nest, as orbit, as a second body, as evacuated intelligence, as a lasting onset of impulse, as radiance, snugglebunny, as friend, protection and as shield, as magical assistant. As hero. As heaven pelt. Not as substitute. As world.

He had my glasses on and was astonishingly hairy, though that is scarcely astonishing in an ape. Later I lost my glasses. I lost the sentence. I know a lot about love and nothing about sex. Can I really know so much about love then? Or do I really know nothing about sex? I said Yes naturally to anyone who wanted to know that about me, but I thought No. No, I know nothing. I wasn't ashamed to lie. I was ashamed not to lie. I am ashamed of giving way to shifting signals. I should not prefer the vague, I should choose risk, because risk wants me. It takes me. Given. I am ashamed. I tried to clutter words around me like: That is to say, to make a skin or a house, for just as long as it lasted, to let it lull me

Bett betrachtet – wie sich selbst erzählen. Wie kann sterben leben sein, wie sie sagen. Wie kann der Stern dich wissen, und wie wichtig ist das für dich.

Ich habe einen neuen Engel: den Affen. Er erschien mir in Vals. Ich habe. Ich habe nicht. Ein Mönch denkt so nicht. Ich bin kein Mönch, ich sollte mich dafür nicht schämen. Ich sollte mich schämen, wie ein Mönch sein zu wollen. Ich will es nämlich nicht. Der Affe aus Vals ist schlau. Er sagte etwas, was ich nie vergessen wollte, nachdem ich mich in seine Arme vergrub. Natürlich wusste ich, dass ich einen Affen verloren hatte und selbst einen bilden sollte in mir, in dem ich schlafen will. Nicht für immer. Ein Affe als Nest, als Umlaufbahn, als zweiter Körper, als ausgelagerte Intelligenz, als stabiler Triebansatz, als Ausstrahlung, Kuschelfeld, als Freund, Schutz und als Schild, als Zaubergehilfe. Als Held. Als Himmelsfell. Nicht als Ersatz. Als Welt.

Er hatte meine Brille auf und war erstaunlich haarig, obwohl das bei Affen nicht erstaunlich ist. Später verliere ich meine Brille. Ich habe den Satz verloren. Ich weiss viel von der Liebe und nichts von Sex. Kann ich dann viel von der Liebe wissen? Oder weiss ich dann nichts von Sex? Ich sagte natürlich Ja zu jemand, der das von mir wissen wollte, dachte aber Nein. Nein, ich weiss nichts. Ich schämte mich nicht zu lügen. Ich schämte mich, nicht zu lügen. Ich schäme mich, auszuweichen ins Verschieben von Zeichen. Ich sollte nicht das Vage, ich sollte Wagnis wollen, weil es mich nämlich will. Es nimmt mich. Bestimmt. Ich schäme mich. Ich versuchte,

to sleep, a postponement, the time left till: me. Betweenstar.

I was ashamed not to know if it is not just exactly this, nothing, that you can know about sex. She was old enough. When I love somebody, it is the person I'm going to lose next. So what do I know about love? I know a lot about loss. Am I obsessed? Whoever is stuck in the tunnel, is systematically stuck in concealment, temporarily out on loan maybe, lost, put at the disposal of the earth and its hopelessness, so the earth can express itself and work it out in the all-too-knowing field. I explode. I implode. Don't stuff yourself full on me.

Long ago as I child in the bathroom I imagined expression and impression, behind milk glass panes, like the feeding of the new baby and with big commotion about the process required to lead to human beings, about the flesh that's involved and the possibility of the absence of love, thoughts or some beauty or at least some consolation during the whole business going on down there in the abdomen.

You suck all the suffering out of love, you even try to feast on the dry hulls, heroine of love pain, he wrote, he who himself is no longer in the position of love, to commit yourself so hopelessly, you teenager. So you really didn't get it, he writes, when she asks if love for him is like abandonment. He is always an other. You aren't it. You read it. You write it. Men don't stay. Never, he writes. Yes? You know, everything flows.

Wörter als Haut oder Haus um mich herumzumullen, zum Beispiel: nämlich, mich solange es dauert, von ihm einlullen lassen, ein Aufschub, Frist bis zum: ich. Zwischenstern.

Ich schämte mich, nicht zu wissen, ob es nicht das ist, nichts, was du von Sex wissen kannst. Sie war alt genug. Wenn ich jemanden liebe, ist es der Mensch, den ich als nächstes verliere, was weiss ich dann von der Liebe? Ich weiss viel von Verlust. Bin ich verbohrt? Wer im Tunnel steckt, ist in die Verborgenheit gesteckt, vorübergehend ausgeborgt vielleicht, verliehen, doppelt verloren, der Erde und der Ausweglosigkeit zur Verfügung gestellt, damit sie sich ausdrückt, abreagiert im allzu wissenden Feld. Ich bin übertragen. Ich explodier. Ich implodier. Fress dich nicht satt an mir.

Ich habe mir Ausdruck und Eindruck früher im Badezimmer vorgestellt, hinter Milchglasscheiben, wie die Fütterung des neuen Babys und mit grosser Empörung über den notwendigen Vorgang, der zu Menschen führt, über das involvierte Fleisch dabei und die Möglichkeit des Fehlens von Liebe, Gedanken oder irgendwas Schönem oder wenigstens Tröstlichem während des Vorgangs im Gekröse.

Du saugst aus der Liebe alles Leid, noch an den trockenen Schoten versuchst du dich zu laben, Heldin der Liebespein, schreibt er, der sich selbst der Liebe nicht mehr in der Lage ist, sich so rettungslos zu verschreiben, schreibt er, du Teenager. So ist es nun auch wieder nicht, schreibt er, als sie fragt, ob Liebe bei ihm gleich Verlassen ist. Er ist immer ein anderer.

He is proud of being a man who dares to leave a woman, a woman he has in several respects not stopped loving. That is strong. Aura of ow-autonomy. Shame of having connected with someone who is not deeply connected with you. For being out of synch. Bad angle. The side is crooked. Lack of symmetry. Not much of an arrangement. *One sided love.* The heart struck + at the same time pierced through with a tool, like a death's head now, dripping. Imprecise intimacy. Cheat. Let go of what doesn't want to be with you. And me myself? To stay too long is too terrible. The corpse smells bitter then. It's the amount of loss that screams.

The monk says, that's just ego. Sorrow is dirt, ego says, you are worthless. No one would get rid of something valuable. You are superfluous. The thing that is valuable about you is your disappearance. When you've disappeared. She might be appetizing if he doesn't want anything of her. He doesn't want to separate from his own will, so he is separating from her, who wants to separate him from his will.

Can you tell need from lust. He wanted to work his will on his wife. Does this mean Wollust? *Does this mean he wanted her and himself to be overwhelmed by* Wollust *without touching? Which touching? Moving without moving is* Wollust? *Do I want lust?*

Or is it just eternity? Is this what she should urgently know about sex? Is she ashamed of being innocent? Is innocence beyond a certain age perverse? In Gottlieben I saw three

Du bist es nicht. Du liest es. Du schreibst es. Männer bleiben nicht. Nie, schreibt er. Ja? Du weisst ja, es fliesst.

Er ist stolz darauf, ein Mann zu sein, der eine Frau verlässt, die er in einigen Punkten nicht aufgehört hat zu lieben. Das ist stark. Aura der Auaautonomie. Scham, dich mit wem verbunden zu haben, der nicht innig mit dir verbunden ist. Für die Ungleichzeitigkeit. Falscher Winkel. Krumme Schenkel. Mangel an Symmetrie. Wenig schöne Ordnung. One sided love. Das Herz getroffen + dabei durchgestrichen mit einem Werkzeug, wie Totenkopf, der tropft. Ungenaue Innigkeit. Trug. Lass gehen, was nicht bei dir sein will, und ich selbst? Zu lange bleiben ist zu furchtbar. Die Leiche riecht dann bitter. Es ist die Summe der Verlorenheit, die schreit.

Der Mönch sagt, es ist nur Ego. Schmerz ist Schmutz, sagt Ego, du bist wertlos. Niemand wird Wertvolles loswerden wollen. Du bist überflüssig. Das Wertvolle an dir ist dein Verschwinden. Wenn du verschwunden bist. Sie sei geniessbar, wenn er nichts von ihr wolle. Er sei von seinem Willen nicht zu trennen, deshalb trenne er sich von ihr, die ihn von seinem Willen trennen wolle.

Can you tell need from lust. He wanted to work his will on his wife. Does this mean: Wollust? Does this mean he wanted her and himself to be overwhelmed by Wollust without touching? Which touching? Moving without moving is Wollust? Will ich Wollust?

male swans who while they were mounting the female kept biting her on her swan neck already bitten bloody, and Swiss women were tossing bread to them. I am ashamed of not having thrown a stone at the Swiss women. Shame distances. I love the openness of lost people, their soft places, their defenselessness. How far away they are. Their sudden resurfacing. Their untouchedness. Their uncontainability, and how they blossom so mightily. I love my empathy with lost people and how I get into their skins, as if I were them. How I feel them inwardly, how I lose myself in them, how I take them to the cemeteries in front of ducks on the steps of the pond, the tattooed people too, who cry because they look at themselves untouched, back and forth and from far away, because I really love to be this way when I love, and once again the will has disappeared. That's it. The gardeners walk by us in rows without whistling, although we're wearing skimpy blouses. The woman asks if we've lost the Frenchman and are waiting for the pageant at the mass grave.

I see you touching me between the shoulders from behind. You call me from in front of me, you tell me come to thee. I see you above me and how they want to spread in flight and I can't fly. I'm ashamed of that, of being called, of being touched. I have lost my will. Deliberately. My will conglomerated with my force of gravity. My will hangs from my neck and my joints. My brother plans his day according to the sun. At the correct time he climbs up the correct hill in the correct light. He wants to get something

Or is it just eternity. Is this what she should urgently know about sex? Schämt sie sich, unschuldig zu sein? Ist Unschuld ab einem bestimmten Alter pervers? In Gottlieben sah ich drei Schwäne, die, während sie eine Schwänin bestiegen, diese in den bereits blutig gebissenen Schwanenhals bissen, und Schweizerinnen, die Brot dazu warfen. Ich schäme mich, keinen Stein auf die Schweizerinnen geworfen zu haben. Scham entfernt. Ich liebe die Offenheit der Entfernten, ihre weichen Stellen, ihre Wehrlosigkeit. Wie sie verloren sind. Ihr plötzliches Auftauchen. Ihre Unberührtheit. Ihre Hemmungslosigkeit und wie sie heftig blühen. Ich liebe meine Einfühlsamkeit in Entfernte und wie ich ihnen unter die Haut geh, als sei ich es selbst. Wie ich sie von innen her fühle, mich verliere, wie ich sie auf Friedhöfe vor Enten in Teichen auf Treppen bringe, auch Tätowierte, die weinen, weil sie auf sich ohne Berührung blicken, nach hinten und vorne und auch von weitem, weil ich so am liebsten bin, wenn ich liebe, schon wieder ist der Wille weg. Das ist es. Die Gärtner gehen in Reihen an uns vorbei ohne zu pfeifen, obwohl wir Hemdchen tragen. Die Frau fragt, ob wir den Franzosen verloren haben und auf das Spektakel am Massengrab warten.

Ich sehe dich mich zwischen den Schultern berühren von hinten und von vorne rufen, ich soll zu dir kommen. Ich sehe dich über mir und wie sie sich ausbreiten wollen zum Flug und wie ich schon wieder nicht fliege. Dafür schäme ich mich. Ich habe meinen Willen verloren. Absichtlich. Mein Wille hat sich in meine Schwerkraft geballt. Mein Wille hängt mir am Hals und an den Gelenken. Mein Bruder plant den Tag nach

out of life. I'm ashamed of not knowing anything about life. Not wanting to learn its rules. // *His rules.* // Don't want to learn the bus timetable. Open hours at the library. I am the kind that wanders around inside myself looking for a screwdriver for the bedroom window that's stuck shut. That's why dreams logically drive me back. They hurt my tail bone and shout: Look for the screwdriver in the daytime world, dork. Every rule that I wound whips around and gives me a venomous bite in the leg. So by now I call my leg Viper. But I'm ashamed of not wanting to learn, since I'm afraid of getting even dumber.

I'm ashamed that I don't believe that you're ashamed you were born. Is the stress on 'born?' The process? That I would understand. In the museum there's a rump with legs outspread and an oval upholstered hole between them for doctors to practice on. I'm ashamed when I see people stand in front of the showcase and see that I can lie down on my back and have something taken out or stuffed in. Again and again I'm the chicken, and a cock betrays me between the chicken coop and Golgotha on the cross in union with // *kisses and cushions* //.

Not to be a soul? Soul in flesh clothes. // *Flesh clover. False clover. Shamrock.* // No animal is ashamed of its form. To be ashamed of not being an animal is perfect. I'm not ashamed I don't believe the thing about the animal. I'm ashamed of the material I am, and for the incomprehensible that I am not, because it should be Light and not so dark, much

der Sonne. Er steigt zum richtigen Zeitpunkt auf den richtigen Hügel ins richtige Licht. Er will was vom Leben haben. Ich schäme mich, das Leben nicht anzuerkennen. Seine Regeln nicht kennenlernen zu wollen. Nicht die Busfahrpläne. Öffnungszeiten der Bibliotheken. Ich bin dieser Typ, der nach innen wandert, um dort den Schraubenzieher für das verschlossene Schlafzimmerfenster zu finden. Deshalb schlagen logisch die Träume zurück. Sie verletzen mein Steissbein und schreien: Such den Schraubenzieher in der Tagwelt, Dussel. Jede Regel, die ich verletze, kehrt sich um und pinkelt giftig an mein Bein. Deshalb nenn ich mein Bein schon mal Viper. Doch ich schäme mich, nicht lernen zu wollen, weil ich Angst habe, davon dümmer zu werden.

Ich schäme mich, dir nicht zu glauben, dass du dich schämst, geboren zu sein. Ist die Betonung auf «geboren»? Der Vorgang? Das verstünde ich. Im Museum ist ein Rumpf mit angewinkelten Beinen und ovalem gepolsterten Loch dazwischen zum Üben für Ärzte. Ich schäme mich, wenn ich Menschen sehe, die vor der Vitrine stehen und sehen, dass ich auf dem Rücken liegen kann und ausgenommen werden oder gestopft. Immer wieder bin ich das Huhn, und ein Hahn verrät mich zwischen Hühnerhof und Golgotha am Kreuz in Einheit mit alten Flammen.

Keine Seele zu sein? Seele im Fleischrock. Kein Tier schämt sich für die Gestalt. Sich zu schämen, kein Tier zu sein, ist perfekt. Ich schäme mich nicht, dir das mit dem Tier nicht zu glauben. Ich schäme mich für das Material, das ich bin, und

163

dirtier than shitty buttocks or inky fingers. I don't believe that at every sentence you speak people vanish out of you. They never vanish, except that they went walking around through you. Once imprisoned in you, they don't walk around with your words out of your mouth, never. The way out, for all the many people who sink in you and sink in me, is loss. When you lose. Loss is infectious. Loss is a slippery slope for loss. Loss is a horror trip for the ego and a Mecca for the soul, my psychiatrist tells me I am like this. Loss of self. *Or is it about inhaling and exhaling?* I am ashamed because I believe everything in reality. I am addicted to believing every word.

I once read a book about Tao. I was supposed to read it by a man who speaks with God. I tried this Tao thing and terrible things happened and heaven happened too. I am ashamed that I want to save myself. My will has vanished into art, I say deliberately, the mother doesn't want that, maybe for that reason. He calls the Tao thing seeing green. He says, that is the title. It has this idea. Seeing green, sowing green, sea green. I pretend, as if I'm able to do it. But I can't do it. I can't. Knowledge is fleeting, it can't be held. Holding is knowing. Please hold me. Art is a holder, and is naturally filthy.

Are people who are afraid to flow too much people who have lost their core? What do they do when they've lost their core, when they arrive at the middle of love in the middle of themselves and there's no core there? Distancing

für das nicht Fassbare mit den Händen, das, was ich nicht bin, weil es Licht sein sollte und nicht so dunkel, viel schmutziger als dreckige Backe oder Tintenfinger. Ich glaube nicht, dass bei jedem Satz, den du sprichst, Leute aus dir verschwinden, wie du sagst. Sie verschwinden nie, ausser sie gingen durch dich hindurch. Sie spazieren nicht mit deinen Worten aus deinem Mund heraus, wenn sie einmal in dir einsitzen, niemals. Der Ausweg für die vielen Leute, die in dich sinken, und in mich, ist Verlust. Wenn du verlierst. Verlust ist ansteckend. Verlust ist eine rasende Rutschbahn für Verlust. Verlust ist ein Horrortrip für das Ego und ein Mekka für die Seele, sagt mein Psychiater zu mir, ich sei so für dich und für jeden. Selbstverlust. Or is it about inhaling and exhaling? Ich schäme mich, weil ich dir alles glaube in Wirklichkeit. Ich bin süchtig danach, jedes Wort zu glauben.

I once read a book about Tao. I was supposed to read it by a man, who speaks with God. I tried this Tao thing and terrible things happened and heaven happened too. Ich schäme mich, dass ich mich retten will. Mein Wille ist verschwunden in die Kunst, sage ich mutwillig, die Mutter will das nicht, vielleicht deshalb. Er nennt das Taoding: Grün sehen. Er sagt: Das ist der Titel. Es hat diesen Sinn. Grün sehen. Grün säen. Grünsee. Ich tue so, als ob ich so tuen könnte. Ich kann aber nicht. Ich kann nicht. Das Wissen ist ja flüssig, es ist nicht zu behalten. Behalten ist ja wissen. Bitte behalte mich. Kunst ist Behälter und natürlich schmutzig.

Sind Menschen, die fürchten, zu sehr zu fliessen, entkernt?

165

is there. I am ashamed of this business of the core. A person as a fruit. As a pumpkin. For clumsiness, for the curse of having to explain, for penetrating into your soul. The tragedy of communication, invading your territory. I am ashamed that my soul betrothed itself with yours involuntarily, and that I enter under your roof, where I blossom. I didn't walk under your roof, I was there already, I couldn't not know it any longer. I am lost.

Did I want to be loved by you as a monk would love me, as if I were clover in the field. The man I love perhaps possesses this ability, to love clover. Only I don't know how a clover is supposed to handle this lust business. *Shamrock*. White clover is one possibility for embodiment without the zone of shame, without flesh. Soul in clover attire. *I can't tell flower from Birgit*. Romantic and false. I don't come to myself. I'm not in the current. I can't be left standing in love in the field. Every flower can do what I can't do. I can't be left standing in love in the field. I can. That I can do. I can be left. When I'm left, I'm a plant, I can't run away. Even if I call my legs vipers, that stand in their own venom, catatonic. I can be catatonic. I can be mowed down. Torn up. Grow low. You see, this is someone who doesn't know the world. In me there are no monks who lovingly observe the marked-out field. In me there is no field marked out. I am stuck in the field. I totter. In me there are murderers. (There it is, your name: Moses. There it is, the basket, the magnitudes, the little one in the basket found on the river fair before the Lord the crying child Paul Moses. You are the one. Always.

Was tun denn Entkernte, wenn sie in der Liebe mitten in sich in ihre Mitte geraten und da ist Entkernung. Entfernung ist da. Ich schäme mich für das mit dem Kern. Der Mensch als Frucht. Als Kürbis. Für die Plumpheit, für den Fluch des Erklärens, für das Eindringen in deine Seele dabei. Die Tragödie der Kommunikation, in dein Territorium dringen. Ich schäme mich, dass sich meine Seele mit deiner unwillkürlich vermählte, und dass ich eingehe unter deinem Dach, wo ich blühe. Ich bin nicht unter dein Dach spaziert, ich war schon da, ich konnte es nicht länger nicht wissen. Ich bin verloren.

Wollte ich von dir wie von einem Mönch geliebt werden, als wär ich ein Feldklee. Der Mann, den ich liebe, hat diese Fähigkeit vielleicht, Feldklee zu lieben. Nur weiss ich nicht, wie ein Feldklee mit dieser Wollustsache zu recht kommen soll. Shamrock. Weisser Feldklee ist eine Möglichkeit der Verkörperung ohne Schambereich, ohne Fleisch. Seele im Kleekleid. I can't tell flower from Birgit. Romantisch und falsch. Ich komm nicht zu mir selbst. Ich bin nicht im Fluss. Ich kann nicht in der Liebe im Feld stehen gelassen werden. Jede Blume kann, was ich nicht kann. Ich werde in der Liebe im Feld stehen gelassen. Ich kann. Das kann ich. Ich kann verlassen werden. Wenn ich verlassen werde, bin ich eine Pflanze, ich kann nicht weglaufen. Auch wenn ich meine Beine Viper nenne, die im eigenen Gift stehen, kataton. Ich kann kataton sein. Ich kann abgemäht werden. Weggerissen. Niederblühen. Da erkennt nämlich jemand die Welt nicht. In mir sind keine Mönche, die liebend das abgesteckte Feld

Never aren't you the one.)

A shame field so excited that it implodes, into another world. In this world it's just clumsiness. *Shame to be such a clumsy cold frog with ugly movements, odd sounds coming uninvited by anybody, unwished, completely unwelcomed out of every hole of your body.* Shame, eternal, always and yet incalculably going in the wrong direction, pull, and you push, *Beziehung* means pulling? Pull and you push. Come, and I remain standing. Never going in harmony in the same direction with anything or anyone. Don't be so in love with harmony, rhythm, that you bite in the calf, yapping, fathoms deep you stand on its feet. Don't be so in love with the wave that you want, the one that moves only without will. The will is always the third. Tri-angel. Tempt the angel. I am ashamed of my relation to it. I'm always ashamed when I say: It doesn't work, over and over.

I am ashamed of not being bright and radiant, not even there where you touch me, if you touch me, of still being dark anyhow, so you go further, heavy as a stone, weighed down with guilt, weighed down shoulders and still to fly up, I'm ashamed: *I fly such high* and look down, I see the girl with the black ringlets from Tenniel's woodcut, how I bind myself, force myself down, press, thrust down, suffering in the earth, never leave it. Yes, that is my will, that makes itself independent, that goes against me, I can do nothing against it, it is itself. Shame is the codeword for will – bewildered, gagged, omnipotent, buried in itself, unholy, never ending,

betrachten. In mir ist kein Feld abgesteckt. Ich stecke im Feld. Ich stocke. In mir sind Mörder. (Da ist er, dein Name: Moses. Da ist es, das Körbchen, die vermisste Grösse, das Kleine im Körbchen treibt auf dem Fluss schön vor Gott der weinende Knabe Paul Moses. Du bist es. Immer. Niemals bist du es nicht.)

So sehr erregtes Schamfeld, das implodiert, in eine andere Welt. In dieser Welt Unbeholfenheit. Shame to be such a clumsy cold frog with ugly movements, odd sounds coming uninvited from anybody, unwished, completely unwelcomed out of every hole of your body. Scham, ewig, immer und doch nicht berechenbar in die falsche Richtung zu gehen, pull, und du drückst, pull heisst Beziehung?, ziehen, und du stösst. Komm, und ich bleib stehen. Nie in dieselbe Richtung mit irgendwas und wem in Einklang zu gehen. Sei nicht so verliebt in den Einklang, den Rhythmus, dem du kläffend in die Waden beisst, klaftertief auf den Füssen stehst. Sei nicht so verliebt in die Welle, die du willst, die nur ohne Willen geht. Der Wille ist immer das Dritte. Triangel. Den Engel versuchen. Ich schäme mich für mein Verhältnis zu ihm. Ich schäme mich immer, wenn ich sage: Es geht nicht, unendlich.

Ich schäme mich, nicht hell und leuchtend zu sein, auch nicht da, wo du mich berührst, wenn du mich berührst, trotzdem dunkel zu sein, weshalb du weiter gehst, steinschwer, beladen mit Schuld, beladenen Schultern, und doch so weit oben zu fliegen, schäme ich mich: I fly such high und nach unten zu sehen, das Mädchen am Boden mit schwarzen Locken von

delirious, unconscious, satanic, divine, godless, fruitless, barbaric, desperate, surrendered to itself, split up in itself. // *Will with a gag in its mouth.* //

Will and core? I am ashamed of not being unconscious, since I would happily fall down in a faint, if it would carry me along, feather in the wind, which belongs to another body in another sphere, *to faint*, fine for me at last, to be with my people at last.

You blow on my shoulder, and I'm ashamed that you don't take my ropes gently out of my hand, the way you do it, what I won't let you do, won't let happen what happens. Shame, that time, when that one wanted to carry you, to throw him off, to jump off, to say: You can't hold me, and this one, when he sketched a picture on the telephone of how he carries you around your room, and this nice picture, constructed for his and your pleasure—pleasure and love are a contrast-pair—you got him so confused with logic and spatial concepts that he lets you go, starts thinking, and look what happened, I fall. I fall when you carry me. Shame of being heavier than the world. I fall through. I touch it. It doesn't work.

I am ashamed, when you breathe, not to believe, to be there, not to allow it. But on the threshold did you lift me up high, and then set me down again, did I hold my breath? Was I really there? I said: You can do it. Didn't I get out on the way up, as he lifted me high? Didn't I climb into all those times

Tanniel, Holzschnitt, wie ich mich fessel, nach unten zwinge, drücke, presse, in die Erde quäle, es nicht lasse. Ja, das ist mein Wille, der sich selbständig macht, der gegen mich geht, ich kann nichts machen gegen ihn, er ist es selbst. Scham ist das Deckwort für Wille. Für verwirrten, geknebelten, omnipotenten, in sich versenkten, heillos ausufernden, sich selbst ausgelieferten, rasend ohnmächtigen, satanischen, göttlichen, gottlosen, fruchtlosen furchtbaren babarischen verweifelten in sich selbst zerstrittenen Willen.

Wille und Kern? Ich schäme mich, nicht ohnmächtig zu sein, weil ich gerne in die Ohnmacht fiele, wenn sie mich trüge, hinweggeblasen wie eine Feder, die an einen anderen Körper einer anderen Sphäre gehört, to faint, endlich vornehm genug für mich, endlich bei meinen Leuten sein.

Du bläst auf meine Schulter, und ich schäme mich, dass du mir meine Stricke nicht leicht aus der Hand nimmst, wie du es tust, was ich dich nicht lasse, es nicht passieren lasse, was passiert. Scham, jenen damals, als er dich tragen wollte, abzuwerfen, abgesprungen zu sein, du kannst mich nicht halten zu sagen, und diesen, als er dir das Bild entwirft, am Telefon, wie er dich trägt durch deinen Raum, ihm das Bild, für deinen und seinen Genuss hingebaut – ist Genuss und Liebe ein Gegensatzpaar –, diesen mit Logik und Raumkonzepten so sehr zu verwirren, dass er dich loslässt, nachdenkt, und siehst du? ich falle. Ich falle, wenn du mich trägst. Scham, schwerer als die Welt zu sein. Ich falle durch. Ich komme auf. Es geht nicht.

171

they wanted to lift me up, when he lifted me up, and had I been in too many upliftings to be there then. Did I dance in blistering shoes? Am I lying? Am I evading? It was much too beautiful for me. I could have gone crazy, it was so beautiful. It is so awful for the ones who are abandoned if even when they were there, they weren't there, because it was too beautiful for them.

It is awful, too, when it is too awful. We meet each other. The middle finger of my right hand starts getting numb. I listen to you. You just crop up. I don't feel anything. I look into your eyes. Nothing happens. I'm an icebox. I know that I feel ashamed about not feeling. My eyes narrow. My feet are cold. Soon I will have to call the ambulance, I tell you, I am dying off. I could have told you that I can't feel anything, I say, and not talk about my finger. You turn dark and sad and I cry and feel ashamed about this. I sit deep in my shame. Shame closes me, and so opens me.

I said: You are not too much for me. I myself am too much. It was on the Persian carpet, on which, if it had gone according to my father's wishes, horses would have been standing. They stamped their feet: *I can't get no satisfaction*, and somebody took me piggyback. Someone else cycled later down to the kiosk and brought me some mineral water, like fetching lettuces in the middle of the night for a pregnant woman. I am ashamed of pretending to you that you carried me. I'm ashamed that I leave myself so that I don't get left by you. There is no shame without loss of

Ich schäme mich, wenn du atmest, nicht zu glauben, da zu sein, es nicht erlauben. Aber, auf der Schwelle, hast du mich hochgehoben, und wieder abgesetzt, hielt ich den Atem an? War ich dabei da? Ich sagte: Du kannst das. Bin ich nicht auf dem Weg nach oben ausgestiegen, als er mich hochgehoben hat? Bin ich in all die Male eingestiegen, als sie mich hochheben wollten, als er mich hochhob, und war in zuvielen Hochhebereien da, um da zu sein? Tanzte ich in glühenden Schuhen? Lüge ich? Lenke ich ab? Es war viel zu schön für mich. Ich hätte wahnsinnig werden können, so schön war es. Es ist schlimm für die Verlassenen, wenn sie, als sie da waren, nicht da waren, weil es zu schön für sie war.

Es ist auch schlimm, wenn es zu schlimm ist. Wir treffen uns. Der Mittelfinger meiner rechten Hand beginnt gefühllos zu werden. Ich höre dir zu. Du zeigst dich. Ich fühle nichts. Ich schau in deine Augen. Es passiert nichts. Ich bin ein Kühlschrank. Ich weiss, dass ich mich schäme dafür. Meine Augen werden schmal. Meine Füsse kalt. Ich muss bald in die Ambulanz, sag ich zu dir, ich sterbe ab. Ich könnte auch sagen, dass ich nichts fühle, sag ich, und nicht vom Finger reden. Du wirst dunkel und traurig und ich weine und schäme mich dafür. Ich sitze in ihr ein. Die Scham schliesst mich ab und öffnet mich dabei.

Ich sagte: Du bist nicht zuviel für mich. Ich bin ja selbst zuviel. Es war auf dem Perserteppich, auf dem, wenn es nach dem Vater gegangen wäre, Pferde stünden. Sie stampften: I can't get no satisfaction, jemand nahm mich Huckepack.

shape or the fear of that.

I am ashamed of my neck, shoulders, collarbone, edges, ligaments, picket fences, moorings, watchmen and knights and hounds and weapons in me, ashamed of not flowing, not flowing, ashamed of stopping. Contrary, you say when you whisper, how you take me on you, put me on top, etc., how you triumph, on the telephone, how you show me, your prey, naked, as he says the gods are looking, you doubted it, that didn't seem right, when he said the gods are looking, and as he undertook the corresponding handling of you with his hand, there took place something that belongs between just the two of you and the gods. It is outrageous. I'm ashamed of being alone with the outrageous and locked in.

The king is not clear. Happiness is not enjoyed. Great danger when the pitcher breaks. Is she ashamed of breaking it? Breaking the pitcher, the king? He is the untouchable, if he wants. If anybody who can be untouchable when he wants is touched and wants it, is he touchable then, or is he someone who is not in touch with the untouchable, if he gets touched and wants it, whether he now wants it or not. No one wants this question.

She writes: I missed you, and means her father. She sends the letter. She says she is ashamed that the words used in love are always the same. Love, every love the same love is like betrayal. For such human laws, that all loves are in one

Jemand anders radelte später deshalb zum Kiosk und brachte mir Sprudelwasser, wie der schwangeren Frau die Rapunzeln mitten in der Nacht. Ich schäme mich, dir vorgetäuscht zu haben, dass du mich trägst. Ich schäme mich, damit du mich nicht verlässt, mich selbst zu verlassen, etc. Es gibt keine Scham ohne Formverlust oder Angst davor.

Ich schäme mich für meinen Nacken, Schultern, Schlüsselbein, Grenzen, Bänder, Stachelzäune, Vertäuungen, Wächter und Ritter und Hunde und Waffen in mir, nicht zu fliessen, nicht zu fliessen, zu stoppen, Widerborst, sagst du, wenn du flüsterst, wie du mich auf dich nimmst, auf die Spitze setzt, etc., wie du triumphierst, am Telefon, wie du mich zeigst, deine Beute, nackt, als er sagte, die Götter schauen zu, daran zweifeltest, das stimmt nicht, als er sagte, die Götter schauen zu, und als er die entsprechende Handlung dazu mit seiner Hand an dir vornahm, passierte, was zwischen euch und die Götter gehört. Es ist unerhört. Ich schäme mich, allein mit dem Unerhörten zu sein und eingesperrt.

Der König ist nicht klar. Das Glück wird nicht genossen. Grosse Gefahr, wenn der Krug bricht. Schämt sie sich fürs Brechen? Den Krug? Den König? Er ist der Unberührbare, wenn er will. Wenn jemand, der unberührbar sein kann, wenn er will, berührt wird und es will, ist er dann berührbar, oder ist er dann jemand, der keine Berührung mit dem Unberührbaren hat, wenn er berührt wird und das will, ob er nun will oder nicht. Niemand will diese Frage.

love, not mixed, unmingled, clearly distinguished, mutually illuminating, that this is right and is not right, cf. espousal. For such raving desire for clarity, even more than for love. If I were in charge, love would be the clearest, even clearer than clarity. She yearns for love. No more. She is ashamed of the defilement of her inner spaces, the logic that results from that. She is ashamed of her search for truth in love, for her cold glance on the lying child she was. She says she is ashamed of her expectations, disappointments, *to be such much disappointed not to be able to admit this, not admitting anything that hurts or even could lead to hurting, like as a child, that denies the car accident, being thrown by the car through the air, ending in a corner, bleeding till night, not able to move, nor to cry, nor to admit this, though your parents can read it in the newspaper tomorrow, they read: Where is the second girl? Not me. I am not.* Even though you can read that. The parents who let you cross that deadly intersection every day to bring the other girl safe to her parents, they are not guilty, says the court, because you were very mature for your age.

Shame of being the one who does it to herself before it happens, does it with scissors, tweezers, pencil, running in front of the car, drowning, telling her father, in his uncomprehending eyes: My eyes did not get wet, over and over untill today, being a human, not an extraterrestrial, who bleeds, has pains and bones — but, *sweetheart*, the soul is big enough for the body, climb in.

Sie schreibt: Ich habe dich vermisst, und meint ihren Vater. Sie schickt den Brief ab. Sie sagt, sie schämt sich, dass die Worte beim Lieben dieselben sind. Liebe, jede Liebe dieselbe Liebe gleich Verrat. Für solche Menschengesetze, dass alle Lieben in einer Liebe sind, nicht vermischt, unvermischt, klar unterschieden, sich gegenseitig beleuchtend, dass dies stimmt und nicht stimmt, siehe Vermählung. Für so viel rasende Sehnsucht nach Klarheit, mehr noch als nach Liebe. Wenn ich verantwortlich wäre, wäre die Liebe das Klarste, noch klarer als die Klarheit. Also sehnt sie sich nach Liebe. Mehr nicht. Sie schämt sich für die Schändung ihrer Innenräume, die daraus resultierende Logik. Sie schämt sich für ihre Sucht nach Wahrheit, in der Liebe, für ihre kalte Sicht auf das lügnerische Kind, das sie war. Sie sagt, sie schämt sich für ihre Erwartungen, Enttäuschungen, to be such much disappointed not to be able to admit this, not admitting anything that hurts or even could lead to hurting, like as a child, that denies the car accident, being thrown by the car through the air, ending in a corner, bleeding till night, not able to move, nor to cry, nor to admit this, though your parents can read it in the newspaper tomorrow, they read: Where is the second girl? Not me. I am not. Obwohl du das lesen kannst. Die Eltern werden freigesprochen vor Gericht, die dich täglich das Mädchen über die tödliche Kreuzung bringen liessen, weil du für dein Alter sehr weit warst.

Scham, die zu sein, die, bevor es passiert, es sich selbst zufügt, mit Schere, Pinzette, Streichholz, vors Auto laufen, ertrinken, dem Vater sagen, in seine fassungslosen Augen: Meine Augen

I am ashamed of writing. Writing is betrayal, since writing is love. That is clear. I am too apollonian for a woman. Where is my cute humiliating passivity. Why can't I be // *pretty and sexy* //. I am ashamed of not letting it change by itself without being affected by me, dragging it into the light, penetrating, not to be pure pleasure, to scorn, to be mistrustful, to stab horrible vicious bloody when I'm scared that someone will stab me, and always coming closer to this own body of mine that can't endure it.

I am ashamed of not being graceful in love, affectionate, docile to the laws of love, not being able to respond to all the systems, sublimities, symmetries and flower stalks, of falling, of stumbling out of the cosmic dances, clumsy footed, crushing flowers underfoot, smelling unclean, I am ashamed of my will, that out of the distance sets itself against me, ashamed of my capacity to move out, to put it in a body, and not be responsible for it. I am ashamed of me, this me that claws at me, holds tight, pushes down, flees into the earth, presses in, stuffs down, treads, tramples, tramples with my heels, when I really want to fly and want to give myself to you, as I see that from up above, as I circle, sway, from high above I look and see how I force myself down, what a burden that is for me and for you.

Haughtily I command myself: leave loss, instead of burdening me, she says, her angel is at the end of patience with her. No, my angel is not on the brink. My angel has a hundred hands and all are full of light, my thoughts don't

sind nicht nass geworden, immer wieder bis heute, ein Mensch zu sein, der kein Ausserirdischer ist, blutet, Schmerzen hat und Knochen, – aber, sweetheart, die Seele ist ja gross genug für den Körper, steig ein.

Ich schäme mich zu schreiben. Schreiben ist Verraten, weil Schreiben Lieben ist. Das ist klar. Ich bin viel zu apollinisch für eine Frau. Wo ist meine schöne beschämende Passivität. Warum kann ich nicht lecker lasziv sein. Ich schäme mich, es sich nicht von mir unangetastet verwandeln zu lassen, es ins Licht zu zerren, darin einzudringen, nicht reines Vergnügen zu sein, zu trotzen, misstrauisch zu sein, grausam böse blutig zuzustechen, wenn ich fürchte, dass mich jemand sticht, und immer näher an diesen eigenen Körper zu kommen, der es nicht ertragen kann.

Ich schäme mich, in der Liebe nicht anmutig, anschmiegsam, den Gesetzen der Liebe gemäss, den Anordnungen, Schönheiten, Symmetrien, Blütenstengeln entlang zu antworten, herauszufallen, aus den kosmischen Tänzen, plumpfüssig, Blumen zertretend, unfein duftend, ich schäme mich für meinen Willen, der sich aus der Entfernung schon gegen mich aufstellt, für die Fähigkeit, auszulagern, zu verleiblichen, nicht verantwortlich dafür zu sein. Ich schäme mich für mich, die mich krallt, festhält, niederstösst, in die Erde flucht, dringt, stopft, tritt, niedertritt, mit der Ferse nachtritt, wenn ich fliegen will und mich dir übergeben, wie ich das von oben sehe, die Stelle, wie ich kreise, schwinge, hoch oben sehe ich, wie ich mich nach unten zwinge, welche

179

fit. Yes, I have an angel. I am astonished. I am not ashamed.

I am Napoleon
PROMISED POP SONG NUMBER TWO

I am the Napoleon of love, an Elba, I've got a bellyache,
of the body, an abandoned god, a calf, that's why she runs
from me, where does it linger, through my fingers, this gold,
            these love things, where I love, nobody
could endure it, snake my house: eat her up, since: love is
            nothing against power
against her, against it, hey, tandaradei, my magic is free, it
            rolls my egg, my life is here and there,
nobody's with me anymore, even if I were a genius of love

I am empty god, I'm called Marie, I am a genius of love
my wall is elephant, stream my land, my back hurts
my coal is my snow, my gold is all here and there
pure my heart, glitters, my master locks me out, here's
            strategy:
eat me, she says, eat me up, she lays out the serpent on the
            elephant, that makes
the way, along the back, the wall is ever more Marie, there's
            nobody

Last das ist für mich und dich.

Hochmütig befehle ich mir: Lass los, statt mich einzuladen,
sagt sie, ihr Engel sei ausser Atem mit ihr. Nein, mein Engel ist
nicht am Rand. Mein Engel hat hundert Hände und alle sind
voll Licht, meine Gedanken passen nicht. Ja, ich habe einen
Engel. Ich staune. Ich schäme mich nicht.

Ich bin Napoleon
PROMISED POP SONG NUMBER TWO

Ich bin Napoleon, der Liebe, ein Elba, mein Magen tut weh
des Leibes, ein verlassener Gott, ein Kalb, deshalb fliesst sie
mir, wo bleibt es, durch die Finger, das Gold, diese
                    Liebesdinger, wo ich liebe, hält es niemand
aus, Schlange mein Haus: iss sie auf, weil: die Liebe ist
                              nichts gegen Macht
gegen sie, hei: tandaradei, mein Zauber ist frei, es rollt
                    mein Ei, mein Leben ist hie
niemand ist mehr dabei, und wär ich ein Liebesgenie

Ich bin leerer Gott, ich heisse Marie, ich bin ein Liebesgenie
meine Wand ist Elefant, Strom mein Land, mein Rücken tut weh
mein Pech ist mein Schnee, mein Gold ist all hie
holdes, mein Herz, blitzt, mein Herr schliesst mich aus,
                              hier Strategie:
iss mich auf, sagt sie, sie legt dem Elefant die Schlange auf,
                              das macht
den Weg, den Rücken lang, die Wand ist immer mehr Marie,
                              es gibt niemand

181

anymore, who knows how to love. I am St Helena, far away
                                                is here nobody
anywhere Africa, magic spell, death is order and that's why
                                        ever and ever your love genius
is sure, my man hurts me and pricks me hard
stings me away from him, blood in the snow, where I stand,
                                                nothing hurts me
nothing will more out she
grammar's gone here or here or

I am gold, mountain, the cock crows, the hen is gone,
                                                betrayal is all here
and whose body there catches fire runs out of the house and
                                                screams, it's nobody
burning, storms against the wall, elephant, serpent,
                                                grammar's gone she is
the torch, the flag, the light, the tender, the genius of love
fallen in the fields, addicted from head to toe
in the 143 lapis lazulis torn loose around the Eight
                                                scratched into her neck

the splendor, I am your master, beloved, and push you with
                                                force
away from me, your lap burns dramatically bright, flames
                                                and rolls like
it's burning, swelter with delight, 143 this pain
purifie her, the genius of love, cloak, hell, grotto, grammar,
                                                like nobody
loves her, the love genius

mehr, der die Liebe kann. Ich bin St. Helena, fern ist hier
                                                    niemand
irgendwie Afrika, Bann, Tod ist die Ordnung und daran ewig
                                    immer dein Liebesgenie
sicher, mein Mann tut mir weh und sticht mit Macht
mich von sich, Blut im Schnee, wo ich steh, nichts tut mir
                                                    mehr weh
nichts wird mehr aus sie
hin die Grammatik, hie hie

Ich bin Gold, der Berg, der Hahn kräht, die Henne ist hin,
                                    Verrat ist all hie
und wessen Leib da entfacht aus dem Haus rennt und
                                    schrie, ist niemand
der brennt, gegen Wand, Elefant, Schlange anrennt, hin die
                                    Grammatik ist sie
die Fackel, die Fahne, die leichte, die zarte, das Liebesgenie
gefallen im Feld verfallen von Kopf bis zum Zeh
in die 143 Lapislazuli gerissen los um die in den Hals
                                    geritzte Acht

die Pracht, ich bin dein Meister, Geliebte, und stoss dich
    mit Macht
von mir ab, dein Schoss brennt dramatisch licht, loh und
                                    kullert wie
der brennt, vor Wonne vergeh, 143 dieses Weh
läutere sie, das Liebesgenie, den Mantel, die Höhle, die Grotte,
                                    Grammatik, wie niemand
liebt sie, das Liebesgenie

183

I call Moses, Paul Pot and never love her

I am elephant, the wall with the snake on it, I see her
in front of the house, blossoming in baskets, and take her by
force

nothing happens, we are in love's genius
in the house are we never and anywhere
Afghanistan, she won't eat the snake and I want to love
nobody

anywhere, I want pain right now

the wall breaks, she is the genius of love
people scream, she strikes them down, in striking she
screams: force

never again, she becomes lapis lazuli

Shame. Mash. Terrible. Shameless sh sound. Obscene.
Sludge. Toad. Sh pierces the body, splashes out of it. *Hush
hush little baby*. Sh regression. Farting. Sucking. To have a
body is a scandal. A body that wants to be touched. Held.
Never again show body or let it be touched. Mucus
membrane. Eyes, that pour. The breath after sleeping, drag
out, brushing your teeth in the night. When he kisses you
where his semen is. Slobbering in sleep. The chin falls on
the chest. The nose snores. The pillow is damp. Traces on
the sheet. People make sh-stuff. The body is not the shame
thing, it's the inability, the fear, not letting go, not the
thought, not the wish, not the wanting, to depend on it, on
the body, to be unfree, to depend on the whole body of the

ich heisse Moses, Paulpott und liebe nie sie

Ich bin Elefant, die Wand mit der Schlange darauf, ich sehe sie
vor dem Haus, blühe im Körbchen und nehm sie mit
                                                    Macht
nichts wird, wir sind in der Liebe Genie
im Haus sind wir nie und irgendwie
Afghanistan, will sie die Schlange nicht essen und ich will
                                          irgendwie niemand
lieben, ich will sofort Weh

Die Wand bricht, sie ist das Liebesgenie
Leute schreien, die sie erschlägt, im Schlagen schreit sie:
                                          macht
das nie wieder, sie wird Lapislazuli

Scham. Masch. Schrecklich. Schamlose Sch-laute. Obszön.
Matschig. Krötig. Sch dringt in den Körper, platzt aus ihm
raus. Husch husch little Baby. Sch-Regression. Furzen.
Nuckeln. Körper haben ist Skandal. Körper, der berührt
werden will. Gehalten. Nie wieder Körper zeigen oder zum
Anfassen geben. Schleimhäute. Augen, die quellen. Atem nach
dem Schlafen, raus schleichen, Zähneputzen in der Nacht.
Wenn er dich küsst, wo sein Samen ist. Beim Schlafen
sabbern. Das Kinn fällt auf die Brust. Die Nase schnorchelt.
Das Kissen ist nass. Spuren auf dem Laken. Menschen
machen Sch-Sachen. Der Körper ist nicht das Schamding, die
Unfähigkeit ist es, die Angst, nicht loszulassen, das Denken
nicht, das Wünschen nicht, das Wollen nicht, an ihm zu

other person, unfree, unclean, chains, tentacles, jellyfish, ballast, lead shoes, in love and not letting go, to spoil your fun because of this, to be very ashamed not light enough to love and not to love lightly and still be light.

That you jabbed your finger bloody with the tweezers you pierced the tube with in the hotel basement, because you're coming from the train and he's waiting for you in bed with a view of the tracks, he's in white pants, you haven't touched him yet, as if you didn't know what was happening, coming bleeding into his room, doing everything yourself, getting ready, the blossoming, him, before it begins, making him look in his travel kit, bandaids, scissors, matches, no rubbers, you're ashamed about that, because you needed to brush your teeth, go into his room and make love to him, admit it, that you kiss him, because you know it. It would have been so much simpler if you had looked at him and he had said whatever was to be said, but instead he said, because you brought your confusion to bed with you: I knew it was going to be awful with you. I'm ashamed that I shouldered the awfulness for you, that I didn't leave it with you, that I wanted to love you so much, because I love you so much, that I acted against myself but kept it hidden from myself.

You're ashamed because you're crazy. Not pretty. The Graces lost. The gracefulness. Because you're not self-forgetting. Since the man who looks at you doesn't love you, how are you supposed to forget yourself then. I am

hängen, am Körper, unfrei sein, am ganzen Körper unfrei unfein am Anderen dran hängen, unbarmherzige Klette, Tentakelarme, Qualle, Ballast, Bleigestell, in der Liebe nicht loslassen, dir den Spass verderben deshalb, sich sehr schwer schämen, nicht leicht zu lieben zu sein und nicht leicht zu lieben und doch leicht zu sein.

Dass du dir den Finger blutig stichst mit der Pinzette, mit der du im Keller im Hotel die Tube aufstichst, weil du vom Zug kommst und er im Bett mit Blick auf die Gleise auf dich wartet, in weissen Hosen, den du noch nicht berührt hast, als wüsstest du nicht, was passiert, blutend in sein Zimmer kommen, alles selber machen, das Blühen, ihn, bevor es beginnt, in seinen Reisebeutel sehen lassen, Pflaster, Schere, Feuer, Gummi nicht, dafür schämst du dich, weil du Zähne hättest putzen können, in sein Zimmer gehen und ihn lieben, es zugeben, dass du ihn küsst, weil du es weisst. Noch einfacher wäre gewesen, du hättest ihn angesehen und er hätte gesagt, was zu sagen ist, er sagte aber, weil du die Verwirrung mit ins Bett gebracht hast: Ich wusste, dass es schlimm wird mit dir. Ich schäme mich, dass ich dir das Schlimme abgenommen habe, dass ich dich so sehr lieben wollte, weil ich dich so sehr liebe, dass ich gegen mich vorgegangen bin und es aber vor mir verborgen habe.

Du schämst dich, weil du verdreht bist. Nicht schön. Die Grazie verloren. Die Anmut. Weil du nicht selbstvergessen bist. Weil der, der dich sieht, dich nicht liebt, wie sollst du dich da vergessen. Ich schäme mich, nicht geliebt zu sein, das

ashamed of not being loved, of wanting the impossible of me, having been loved. I see myself in an orgy of observation. I see how the atheist father's attempt at coitus interruptus failed, the traces of semen on the thighs of the Catholic mother, on her — and in great terror as the punishment of hell for premarital, and what is more nonproductive, sexual intercourse — the Pope was called Paul — in the shame of the mother, I know it, I am too excited, to say it simply: me. Me beginning. Every interrupted coitus reminds me of me. Coitus or me? False. Utterly false. The other way round.

// *Ach Rilke liebe ich sehr*
ROBERTS ALTERNATIVER POP SONG GEGEN NUMMER DREI

Ach Rainer René Renée
ich liebe dich sehr
du hast entdeckt
ja, nein du hast erfunden
die intersexuelle Sprache
womit die Engel
der Hadith reden
und reden mit uns
the sorry glory
of some old story
religion religion

Santa Maria Formosa

Unmögliche von mir zu wollen, geliebt worden sein. Ich sehe mich in einer Beobachtungsorgie. Ich sehe, wie dem atheistischen Vater im Büschchen der Unterbruch vom Koitus misslang, die Samenspur auf den Schenkeln der katholischen Mutter, auf der – und im grossen Schreck als Höllenstrafe für vorehelichen, zusätzlich zwecklosen Sexverkehr – der Papst hiess Paul – in der Scham der Mutter, ich weiss ja, ich bin zu aufgeregt, um es einfach zu sagen: ich. Beginnendes Ich. Jeder unterbrochene Koitus erinnert mich an mich. Koitus oder ich? Falsch. Ganz falsch. Umgekehrt.

O Rilke I hate you
Birgit's Promised Pop Song Number Three

O Rilke I hate you
as much as I can
I kill you each night
while I wait for my man

he, who made me love him
in order to leave me, he
who left me in order to teach me, he
in order to be me, me, steeped in, deep in
the sorrow and loneliness of the world
he knows nothing about me, but is me
right in the middle I am in, I am he, in

the hell of your smell

ich kniete mich
ich betete
an die Heiligen Lucia
meiner Augen wegen

und dort die Engel
was hören sie nun
nach soviel Dichtung
doch sie reden
sie liebkosen
meine verletzliche Ohrhaut
ich fürchte mich
o Renée René Rainer
Renatus Renata
was für ein Girl du bist
ich fürchte mich
von deinem Gold und Elfenbein
mit Smaragd mit Brustmilch
mit Gondeln
du zwangst
die tote Katze singt
die verbrannte Kirche
schmelzt, sie füllt sich mit Augenwachs
mit Priestersamen mit Nard
Kerzen Zitronen Wein
freilich Wein
du zwangst du zwangst

ich höre ich würde

I am lost in the lust
you laugh: such pretty pain
is just dust, oh shame, and you
Master Rilke, you told him, my man
fucking Rilke
you Rainer Maria

with your tricky poem
in the name of Jesus
Maria Magdalen,
in the name of the masters
who take women like mars dust
to send them in longing and crying
these love denying monsters
who love women's disasters
und wars das?
oh Rilke I hate you, you told all these men

as only a fucking
double name
non fucking love ascetic, love-asshole
love-escaper, a love-overwhelmer
love anti-hero, an artist, a writer, fantastic sublimater
a womeneater and Schlangenfrassbereiter
heroic angel of shame
can do it
I hate you Rilke,
and suck your bad blood
out of each man

dich lesen
du schämst dich nie und nimmer
immer gracilis und unbedingt und reichenarm
nimmer jamais und frische nowhere
Traumdampf aus Ozeandampfer
Frauen
jede Seele ist eine Frau
bei dir jedes Wort ein Scham
du schämst dich niemals
mich zu entverzaubern. //

Ancient ghost law: Whoever doesn't say Yes to one's own dismemberment will never come together again. Ancient spiritual law: *Never is never a condition within our reach.* Three propositions: 1. Will is the other side of lust. 2. Lust is the will to dissolution. 3. Dissolution wants nothing. Beautiful. The course of love: The Delightful. The Tearing to pieces. But why haven't you torn me to shreds. Why do you lack only what dismembers me.

Some spiritual shame. Some backdrwan semen. I am not a man. Amen. I am ashamed of such jokes. Of language. Of human spirit. Of female brain. Am I ashamed of not being a man? As a man, I would love with all my manhood, tender and strong, my heart would show me my way through my penis straight into my love. I would take her and give me, such easy as that. As a woman love is different. As a woman I would not be the churchman in the christmasnight blessing you with the words: Peace and spirit for your body and soul and with

that you and your kind
never again
can write such bloody stuff
this killing pain
Bloody Maria, Rainer, Rilke,
three of them
get out of my vein

Altes Geistergesetz: Wer nicht Ja zur eigenen Zerstücklung sagt, wird nicht wieder zusammengesetzt. Altes Geistgesetz: Never is never a condition within our reach. Drei Sätze: 1. Der Wille ist die andere Seite der Wollust. 2. Die Wollust ist der Wille zur Auflösung. 3. Die Auflösung will nichts. Schön. Liebesablauf: Das Hinreissende. Das Zerreissende. Warum aber hast du mich nicht zerrissen. Warum fehlst du nur, was mich zerreisst.

Some spiritual shame. Some backdrawn semen. I am not a man. Amen. I am ashamed of such jokes. Of language. Of human spirit. Of female brain. Am I ashamed of not being a man? As a man I would love with all my manhood, tender and strong, my heart would show me my way through my penis straight into my love. I would take her and give me, such easy as that. As a woman love is different. As a woman I would not be the churchman in the christmasnight blessing you with the words: Peace and spirit for your body and soul and with my hands do the sign, o no, as a woman, I would kiss you on your forehead, right between your brows.

my hands do the sign, o no, as a woman, I would kiss you on your forehead, right between your brows.

If I don't get a child from you, I'll suck your eye in and everything I see will be your child. I am your child. I am your hip. I am this drawing that you are, from behind, I see your head through your legs from down below. I am this sideways glimpse of you, who got caught, trying to play what it is to get caught. You hustler, I say, you little whore. I see your cruising. How sleazy you are. How professional when you make love and how quick on the mark. How you bind me with your little finger. I am your hands on me. *I am this immense mountain of unbeloved parts, this treasure of unpresent pleasure,* I'll spare you the song // *and dance* //.

The guru has been talking for a year with God. For a year his speech has been ugly. God tells the guru that I should sit in lotus posture, enjoy no sex, and that a woman needs ten years to recover for each child. I am ashamed of the mother murderer in Southend, God told him to kill his mother. Sex or sitting, says the guru, you are not coarse enough for sex if you sit. I'm ashamed because I have no one I can give up sex with, or have, and really huge fear if I did sit and did have. I have. I don't have. We are in me. Who are we in you. I am ashamed of having a damaged guru. I am ashamed of winding bright kerchiefs and colors and love gifts all around you. And he doesn't stand in me. I am ashamed of that. I didn't know that hands flowed from heaven, I didn't know how it is to stand in gold, to be an alchemical object

Wenn ich kein Kind von dir bekomme, sauge ich dein Auge ein und alles, was ich sehe, ist dein Kind. Ich bin dein Kind. Ich bin deine Hüfte. Ich bin diese Zeichnung, die du bist, von hinten, ich sehe deinen Kopf durch deine Beine von unten. Ich bin dieser seitliche Blick von dir, wenn du versuchst, zu spielen, was ist, ertappt sein, der du ertappt bist. Du Stricher, sag ich, du Gassenkind. Ich sehe dein Streunen. Wie verschlagen du bist. Wie professionell, wenn du liebst, und wie auf der Stelle schnell. Wie du mich mit dem kleinen Finger bindest. Ich bin deine Hände an mir. I am this immense mountain of unbeloved parts, this treasure of unpresent pleasure, diesen Song erspar ich dir.

Der Guru spricht seit einem Jahr mit Gott. Seit einem Jahr ist seine Sprache hässlich. Gott sagt dem Guru, ich soll im Lotus sitzen, keinen Sex geniessen und dass die Frau pro Kind zur Wiederherstellung zehn Jahre braucht. Ich schäme mich für den Muttermörder in Southend, dem Gott befal, die Mutter zu töten. Sex oder Sitzen, sagt der Guru, du bist für Sex nicht grob genug dazu, wenn du sitzt. Ich schäme mich, weil ich niemanden habe, mit dem ich auf Sex verzichten könnte, oder haben, und aber gross die Angst, nur falls ich sässe und hätte. Ich habe. Ich habe nicht. Wir sind in mir. Wer sind wir in dir. Ich schäme mich, einen beschädigten Guru zu haben. Ich schäme mich, mit bunten Tüchern und Farben und Liebesgaben dich zu umgarnen. Und er steht nicht in mir. Und ich schäm mich dafür. Ich wusste nicht, dass vom Himmel Hände fliessen, ich wusste nicht, wie es ist, im Gold zu stehen, Gegenstand von Alchemie zu sein im Tor, mitten

in the doorway, and meantime to be in the golden rain and use my talents to croak for those lost.

Goat yearning for release, I say to myself, pull this love back pronto but not yourself, but he's the goat, it is the mutual single simple abolition, embedding, emancipation, it would have been possible, Moses murmurs in the basket, if I had radically changed my life. I am ashamed of the word radical. I am ashamed of the human connection to time, it is possible, I know, it is easy, we are it. We are simply trapped in the coordinates and mistake this captivity for ourselves. It is just the wrong century for us, *darling*, you just feed other foxes and fuck others.

I stand under the sky and accuse. I have it again, that urge to come up to people at random from behind and break their necks with the edge of my hand, or smash their larynx from the front.

You've got to learn to do nothing, he says, during sex, do nothing, and goes away, or is it that? Do you always have to learn something? I'm ashamed, in bed with the man who goes away, to be smitten out of the sky in the dream, because of sex, as the guru says, incest, I warn you, because of it you will fall out of the sky like the Dutch woman. The Dutch woman wanted to die, when she fell out of the sky, and she burnt of shame, which was good, she says, what was left of her warns me of sex. I am ashamed of my obedience. Of my dreams. I am ashamed of not being identical. Not

dabei zu sein im gültigen Regen und an der Begabung für die Entfernten zu krepieren.

Erlösungssüchtige Ziege, sag ich zu mir, zieh subito Liebe zurück und nicht dich, doch die Ziege ist er, es ist die gegenseitige einzige einfache Aufhebung, Einbettung, Freisetzung, es wäre möglich gewesen, murmelt Moses im Körbchen, wenn ich mein Leben radikal verändert hätte. Ich schäme mich für sein Wort: radikal. Ich schäme mich für die Menschenbindung an Zeit, es ist möglich, ich weiss, es ist leicht, wir sind es. Wir sind gefangen in Koordinaten und halten die Gefangenschaft für uns selbst. Es ist doch bloss nur das falsche Jahrhundert gerade darling für uns, du fütterst andere Vögel und vögelst andere bloss.

Ich stehe unter dem Himmel und schimpfe. Ich habe das wieder, den Drang, mit der Handkante beliebigen Leuten von hinten den Nacken zerschmettern zu müssen, oder den Kehlkopf krachend von vorne.

Du musst lernen, nichts zu tun, sagt er, beim Sex, du musst nichts, und geht weg, oder ist es das? Musst du immer etwas lernen? Ich schäme mich, im Bett mit dem Mann, der weg geht, im Traum aus dem Himmel geschmissen zu werden, wegen Sex, wie der Guru sagt, Inzest, ich warne dich, du wirst deshalb aus dem Himmel fallen wie die Holländerin. Die Holländerin wollte sterben, als sie aus dem Himmel fiel, und sie verbrannte vor Scham, was gut war, sagt sie, was von ihr übrig blieb, warnt mich vor Sex. Für meinen Gehorsam

with my dreams. Not with sex. Not with the lotus. Not with the sky. Not with my wish to do nothing and be nothing. Or is it the sister on the air hose, they inflate her and send her out into the universe in a space capsule. I can't be ashamed of the universe, too. My grampa is Dutch and ate and drank excessively and is the one whom I loved and therefore I am ashamed of my Gouda-likeness. I am responsible for much too much. For the snake on the back of the elephant on my way. For my ways among the pecking chickens and always this semen thing: *In the New Guinea highlands boys fellate their elders, ingesting the semen so as to grow big and strong,* that's the kind of thing I pick up.

He can only come when he tells me that he can't come any more, he says, then he comes to me, loves me and cries out and I weep and come to him. Who are you? Now I come just once and then never more. Out of what forest did you come here? After I fell obediently out of the sky, I'm someone who sees how the other one hangs on the air hose and gets inflated, I become more inflated, more distant, an unpleasant memory, a lazy reminiscence, teeth fall out, keep repeating without ever winning, I see that the other one is getting more and more other than me, the men hold a council of war, to save her or to use her? One of them—a traitor? a savior?— says you have to fuck the father and hold onto his prick, it is camouflage, it is a pistol and something is red, but what? Will he come out of the dungeon of abandoned deer, sisters and brothers with the fuck trick and save her? Does someone have to knit the

schäme ich mich. Für mein Träumen. Ich schäme mich, nicht identisch zu sein. Nicht mit meinen Träumen. Nicht mit Sex. Nicht mit Lotus. Nicht mit dem Himmel. Nicht mit meinem Wunsch, nichts zu tun und zu sein. Oder ist es die Schwester am Schlauch, die sie aufpumpen und ins Weltall senden in einer Raumkapsel. Ich kann mich nicht noch für den Weltraum schämen. Ich bin für viel zuviel verantwortlich. Mein Opa ist Holländer und ass und trank masslos und ist der, den ich liebte, und also schäme ich mich für das Goudahafte an mir. Für die Schlange auf dem Rücken des Elefanten auf meinem Weg. Für meine Wege an pickenden Hühnern entlang und ewig diese Samensache: In the New Guinea highlands boys fellate their elders, ingesting the semen so as to grow big and strong, dass ich sowas aufpick.

Er kann erst kommen, wenn er sagt, dass er nicht mehr kommt, sagt er, dann kommt er zu mir, liebt mich und schreit sehr, und ich weine und komme zu ihm. Wer bist du? Nun komm ich noch einmal und dann nimmer mehr. Aus welchem Wald kommst du her? Nachdem ich gehorsam aus dem Himmel fiel, bin ich eine, die sieht, wie eine andere am Schlauch hängt und aufgepumpt wird, ich werde aufgeblasener, ferner, schlechte Erinnerung, faules Gedächtnis, Zahnausfall, Wiederholen ohne Gewinn, ich sehe die andere immer mehr anders werden von mir, die Männer Kriegsrat halten, sie zu retten, oder zu gebrauchen? Einer, ein Verräter? ein Retter? sagt, man muss den Vater ficken, und hält sich den Schwanz, es ist Tarnung, es ist eine Pistole und irgendwas ist Rot, aber was? Kommt er raus aus dem Verliess

sweater all the way to the end? And me? I'm ashamed of being in spiritual dithering, weathering, crumbling rock, disconsolate widow, that God gets on my nerves when he commands the mother murderer to murder his mother and tells the guru that there should be no mothers in the world because they have fear in their sex holes, transmit sorrow through their shame, that hinders the ascent of the soul. *Fuck the guru, mama*, this song I spare you, too.

Under my armpits a region of sorrow proliferates. Under yours I have found protection, slumbered under the roof of the fragrant mushroom and bedded my head in your sweet lap and inhaled you all in reserve, as you see. I still breathe. I am ashamed that I cannot stop my breath. I cannot do the simplest thing. I can't stop.

I am ashamed of my dependency, wanting to stroke the parts of shame, falling into beauty when I touch you, in pictures, arches, through art history, where I still know that love is in me and I should be calm, but I lie on the ground and cry, don't want to fall asleep because I'm afraid of waking up and not wanting to live, without you, I won't do it, I can't do it, I break the law of love. Nothing that the beloved does kills the lover. Who can endure that. That's why they kill you, so that you'll learn. You don't learn easy. I am ashamed of not wanting to live. I'm ashamed that I don't give it a shaking, my guru's body, don't know if I'm responsible for him, how the rules go for this kind of love, I don't recognize the saint. *Fucking hell. Heavy heaven.*

der verlassenen Rehe, Schwestern und Brüder, mit dem Ficktrick, und rettet sie? Muss jemand einen Pullover zu Ende stricken? Und mich? Ich schäme mich in spiritueller Verwirrung zu sein, Verwitterung, bröckliges Gestein, trostlose Witwe, dass mir Gott auf die Nerven geht, wenn er dem Muttermörder befiehlt, die Mutter zu morden, und dem Guru sagt, dass es keine Mütter geben soll, weil sie Angst in ihren Geschlechtshöhlen haben, Schmerz weitergeben durch ihre Scham, der den Aufstieg der Seele behindert. Fuck the guru, mama, diesen Song schenk ich dir nicht.

Unter meinen Achseln wuchert ein Schmerzgebiet. Unter deinen hab ich Schutz gefunden, unter dem Dach des duftenden Pilzes geschlummert, meinen Kopf in deinen Schoss gebettet und dich eingeatmet auf Reserve, wie man sieht. Ich atme noch. Ich schäme mich, den Atem nicht anhalten zu können. Ich kann das einfachste nicht. Ich kann nicht aufhören.

Ich schäme mich für meine Anhänglichkeit, Schamteile streicheln zu wollen, in Schönheit zu fallen, wenn ich dich berühre, in Bilder, durch Bögen, durch Kunstgeschichte, wo ich doch weiss, dass die Liebe in mir ist und ich ruhig sein soll, aber auf dem Fussboden liege und weine, nicht einschlafen will, wegen Angst, aufzuwachen und nicht leben zu wollen, ohne dich, ich will nicht, das darf ich nicht, ich verstosse gegen das Liebesgesetz. Nichts, was der Liebste tut, tötet die Liebste. Wer das aushalten kann. Deshalb töten sie dich, damit du das lernst. Du lernst schwer. Ich schäme mich,

Burning body. I ask him: Why are you afraid to love me
honestly, but the question is: Why are you not afraid not to
love me honestly. But the truth is, love hurts and hurt is only
touching and touching is only touching and I do not know
how to stop the breath yet, as I drowned as a child, this was the
way to paradise, I am ashamed to be thrown out of paradise.

SCHAM 14

Ich schäme mich, schlafen zu müssen. Ich versuche, das zu
verbessern, indem ich die Strasse in den Schlaf hinein pflaster
und dann mit architektonischen Meisterwerken bestücke, die
ich jede Nacht zu zeichnen und aufzurichten gezwungen bin.
Der grosse Freimaurertempel auf der unbekannten Avenue in
Downtown Brooklyn zum Beispiel, das gewaltigste Gebäude,
das meine Träume jemals sahen, auf der Südseite (nicht
Nordseite) dieser Avenue, nah an der Strasse, drohend, riesig,
sich kühn gegen den Hügel abhebend. Welcher Hügel? Und
dann der Tempel im neuen Stil mit Namen *Hemispheric
Perpendicular*. Ich versuche, Türme vom Himmel zu hängen.
Manchmal schäme ich mich für den Pomp und Bombast
dieser Gebäude, sie sind immer zu gross. Ich schäme mich, zu
gross für die Welt zu sein.

nicht leben zu wollen. Ich schäme mich, dass ich ihn nicht schüttel, meines Gurus Leib, nicht weiss, ob ich verantwortlich für ihn bin, wie die Regeln dieser Art von Liebe sind, ich erkenne den Heiligen nicht. Fucking hell. Heavy heaven. Burning body. I ask him: Why are you afraid to love me honestly, but the question is: Why are you not afraid not to love me honestly. But the truth is, love hurts and hurt is only touching and touching is only touching and I do not know how to stop the breath yet, as I drowned as a child, this was the way to paradise, I am ashamed to be thrown out of paradise.

SHAME 14

I am ashamed of having to sleep. I try to make it better by paving the road to sleep, then lining it with architectural masterpieces I am forced to design and erect each night. The great Masonic Temple on the unknown avenue in downtown Brooklyn, for example, the most massive building my dreams have ever seen, on the south (not north side) of that avenue, close to the street—impending, vast, bolding back onto the hill. What hill? And then the temple in the new style called Hemispheric Perpendicular. And I try to hang towers from the sky. Sometimes I am ashamed at the magniloquence and bombast of these buildings, always too big. I am ashamed of being too big for the world. Sometimes though it's enough to design a lovely breakfast room and eat a sleepy breakfast in it with pleasant sleepy people helping themselves to finnan haddie, kippers,

Manchmal jedoch reicht es nicht, einen lieblichen Frühstücksraum zu gestalten und mit netten schläfrigen Leuten ein Schlaffrühstück darin zu essen und sich zu finnan haddie, Schrippen und Rührei zu verhelfen, Silberurnen mit starkem norddeutschem Kaffee. Ich schäme mich für was ich möchte, und wie ich die schimmernde Schamallee hinunter schlender mit beschämenden Begierden, jede ein Stein oder ein Zementgebäude, als ob ich alle meine Lieben in Steine verwandelt hätte, wie so ein dementer, rückwärtsgewandter Pygmalion.

Mein Tempel ist voll mit schamvollen Statuen von neuen Göttern und Göttinnen, Gottheiten, die sich für mich schämen, ihren einzigen Diener. Früher war ich ein Freigelassener. Nun aber möchte ich mich von bestimmten Architekturen befreien, Klaustrophobie meiner eigenen Begierden. Ich will den Stein nicht heiraten, doch er ist rund um mich herum. Der Stein spricht zu mir, zu meinen Händen.

Jeder mit auch nur einer Unze Verstand weiss, dass Homer Menelaos ist, ein Dichter, geblendet durch die Liebe. Er schämte sich, Helena zu verlieren, schämte sich, um sie zu kämpfen, schämte sich, sie zurückzubekommen, schämte sich, mit ihr glücklich zu sein in Ägypten. Ägypten, das heisst die Heirat von Gegensätzen. Homer schämte sich, die Poesie war ein Weg, von der Scham zu singen. Ein Weg, sich zu schämen und wenigstens was draus zu machen, nicht einfach im Schlamm rumschlittern und hinfallen, nicht einfach nur

scrambled eggs, a silver urn with strong North German coffee in it. I am ashamed of what I want, and how the shame alley I saunter down towards the sleep shame shimmers with shameful desires, each one a stone or concrete building, as if I had turned all my loves to stone, like some demented backwards turned Pygmalion.

My temple is filled with shameful statues of new gods and goddesses, deities who are ashamed of me, their only servitor. I was a freedman once. Now I want to get free of certain architectures, claustrophobia of my own desires. I don't want to marry stone but the stone is all around me. The stone talks to me, to my hands.

Anybody with an ounce of sense knows Homer was Menelaus, a poet blinded by love. He was ashamed of losing Helen, ashamed of fighting for her, ashamed of getting her back, ashamed of being happy with her in Egypt. Egypt means the marriage of opposites. Homer was ashamed, Poetry was a way to sing about shame. A way to be ashamed and make something of it after all, not just slipping in the mud and falling, not just having someone run away from you. Poetry is embarrassment. Shame. Shame of wanting. Shame of saying so. And since Homer's time it keeps getting worse. So many things to want, to fail to get, to fail to keep. So many answers ill-fitted to their questions. So many approximations. So much shame.

Desire-based systems inculcate ritual disorder. I've never

jemanden haben, der dir weg läuft. Poesie ist Verlegenheit. Scham. Scham, zu wünschen. Scham, es zu sagen. Und seit den Zeiten von Homers wird es schlimmer. So viele Dinge zu wünschen, nicht bekommen können, nicht halten können. So viele Antworten, die schlecht zu ihren Fragen passen. So viel Annäherung. So viel Scham.

Systeme, die auf Begierde beruhen, pflanzen rituell Störungen fort. Diesen Vogel habe ich nie zuvor gehört. Die den Vogel lasen (in Bejing, in Persien), behalten ihre Gefühle für sich. Schreib mit Wasser, wenn die Tinte ausgeht, nur deine Kinder werden den Unterschied bemerken, die grünäugige Tochter von Pasiphae. Ich habe keine Kinder.

Ich bin immer noch ein kleiner Junge, geschockt, beschämt und entsetzt, entsetzt durch die Weise, wie die zarten Erkundungen der Liebe gekidnappt werden von der brutalen Maschinerie der Fortpflanzung. Ich fragte den Wissenschaftler: Könnt ihr Burschen nicht mal endlich die Erotik von der Fortpflanzung trennen, und die Liebe Körper und Geist erkennen lassen und hinter die beiden kommen, und für ein halbes Leben lang verloren zu gehen in den sozio-biologischen Konsequenzen von Empfindungen, Segen, Begierden, Wissen? Es gibt so viele schöne Penetrationen, so viele sehnsüchtige Lücken in Personen, Dingen, Wetter. Der Körper ist Spiel.

Das ist Daath, die versteckte Sphäre auf dem Lebensbaum, das ist das neue Atlantis, wenn der Körper das spirituelle

heard this bird before. Those who have read the bird (in Beijing, in Persia) keep their feelings to themselves. Write with water when you run out of ink, only your children will notice the difference, the green-eyed daughter of Pasiphae. I have no children.

I am still a little boy shocked and shamed and terrified, terrified, by the way the tender inquiries of love get hijacked by the brutal machinery of reproduction. I asked the scientist: can't you kids finally divide the erotic from the reproductive, and let love know the body and the mind and get beyond both, without getting lost for half a lifetime in the socio-biological consequences of sensation, bliss, desire, knowing? There are so many beautiful penetrations, so many yielding gaps in persons, things, weathers. The body is play.

This is the hidden sphere called Daath on the Tree of Life, this is the New Atlantis, when the body becomes a spiritual instrument of earthly pleasure, and awareness is rescued from the machinery from which it only seems to be produced. I am ashamed of wanting this, I am ashamed of my reluctance to join the ordinary dance. I hate that music. Nobody whistles any more, the music gets internalized. Music means obedience. I will not serve.

I am ashamed of having so many shames, and not confessing all of them. There are so many more things of which I'm ashamed, so many, of body and mind, money

Instrument für irdische Freuden und das Bewusstsein aus der
Maschine gerettet wird, die es anscheinend nur produziert.
Ich schäme mich dafür, das zu wollen, ich schäme mich für
meine Verweigerung, mich dem gewöhnlichen Tanz
anzuschliessen. Ich hasse diese Musik. Niemand pfeift mehr.
Die Musik ist internalisiert. Musik heisst gehorchen.
Ich will nicht dienen.

Ich schäme mich, so viele Sorten Scham zu haben, und sie
nicht alle zu bekennen. Es gibt so viel mehr Dinge, für die ich
mich schäme, so viele, Körper und Geist, Geld und Metall
und eine Fledermaus, die im Zwielicht fliegt, die nichts als
eine Maus mit Flügeln ist. Dass sie fliegen kann. Dass ich
nicht fliegen kann. Die Scham wegen dem. Die Scham, willens
zu sein, sich mit Personen und Szenarios in der realen Welt
zufriedenzugeben, die nur schwache Verkörperungen der
Begierden im Inneren Hof sind. Ich schäme mich für meine
Annäherungen.

Ich schäme mich, niemals meine ganze Scham gesagt zu
haben, ich schäme mich, dass ich ins Grab sinken könnte,
ohne meine Begierden kundgetan zu haben. Ich tröste mich
so: Begierde ist ein innerer Verbrennungsmotor, der dieses
Tier antreibt. Aber es ist innerlich. Aber es ist Trost. Aber das
Tier bewegt sich. Und Scham, Scham ist wie das
Schmiermittel, durch das die Begierde, befriedigt, oder halb
befriedigt oder erstickt, in neue Begierde übergeht.

Am meisten schäme ich mich dafür, nicht alles zu sagen. Lass

and metal and a bat flying over at twilight, why he's nothing but a mouse with wings. That he can fly. That I cannot fly. The shame of that. The shame of being willing to settle for persons and scenarios in the real world that are only feeble impersonations of the desires of the Inner Courtyard. I am ashamed of my approximations.

I am ashamed of never having spoken all my shames, ashamed that I may go to my grave with unproclaimed desires. I console myself like this: desire is an internal combustion engine that drives this animal along. But it is internal. But it is a consolation. But the animal does move. And shame, shame is like the lubricant by which one desire, satisfied or half-satsified or stifled, segues into a new desire.

Above all I am ashamed of not saying everything. Leave something unsaid, they say, be a monk or be tacit, they say, leave something to the imagination, they say. But I say I am ashamed of everything I didn't say.

etwas ungesagt, sagen sie, sei ein Mönch oder still, sagen sie, überlasse etwas der Vorstellung, sagen sie. Aber ich sage, ich schäme mich für alles, was ich nicht sage.

SHAME 15

That was in Basle, luxury disease, the steamboat was called somnolence, the doctor said: Do a Hugo. Whoever does a Hugo, sits down in front of a wall and does nothing. The Hugo I knew was called Hans Otto Hügel, the other was a beanstalk of a twit who touched a bulimic Countess Alexandra in the Black Forest in a sexual way, he was supposed to be putting nourishment into a feeding tube in her neck. Women die at the neck, get killed through the throat, if the womb doesn't do it to them by itself, brutally, down below, the womb wanders upward and chokes the voice, hanging escapes suffocation and leads to a peculiar death of the maiden, who is enclosed between two mouths, two necks. The study of Greek figures leads in me to even more sleep. Sleep is legal disappearance. It would have been brave to sit in your body alive and awake in front of the wall. I work, when I sleep, when I wake up, I write it down and we live off that, I said to my child, that was fatal. You could turn into a fetus. I called my weariness weakness, character weakness.

The waking up is terrible. A scrap of paper, folded to make a bird, hits me, the mother had promised her child to read to him, the child waits and can't sleep the whole night and the

SCHAM 15

Das war in Basel, die Luxuskrankheit, der Dampfer hiess
Schlafsucht, der Doktor sagte: Mach den Hugo. Wer den Hugo
macht, setzt sich vor die Wand und macht nichts. Der Hugo,
von dem ich wusste, war Hans Otto Hügel, der andere war
spannenlanger Hansel und berührte eine bulimische Gräfin
Alexandra im Schwarzwald sexuell, der er Nahrung durch den
Schlauch hätte in den Hals stopfen sollen. Frauen sterben am
Hals, werden durch die Kehle getötet, falls es ihnen die
Gebärmutter nicht von unten brutal von selbst besorgt, die
nach oben wandert und damit die Stimme erstickt, das
Erhängen entgeht dem Ersticken und führt zu einem eigenen
Tod der Mädchen, die zwischen zwei Mündern, zwei Hälsen
eingefasst sind und sonst nichts eigenes haben. Das Studieren
griechischer Figuren führte bei mir zu noch mehr Schlafen.
Schlafen ist legales Verschwinden. Es wäre mutig gewesen, bei
lebendigem Leib wach vor der Wand zu sitzen. Ich arbeite,
wenn ich schlafe, wenn ich aufwache, schreib ich es auf: Wir
leben davon, sagte ich meinem Kind, das war fatal. Zum
Fötuswerden. Ich sagte zu meiner Müdigkeit: Schwäche,
Charakterschwäche.

Das Aufwachen ist schlimm. Ein Zettel, zum Vogel gefaltet,
trifft mich, die Mutter hat dem Kind versprochen vorzulesen,

mother sleeps. I passed up no means of getting to sleep when it needed me, enough to make a whole high-rise full of mothers die of shame. I am ashamed so much and so often that I wasn't there and that I fed on you, my own child. Besides, I read you Kafka. At night I crept under your bed and plundered your treasures, your chocolate eggs. I missed you so often and didn't admit it, I cleared out and left you alone, I don't know if I can go on living. You say that you like your name. You came with this name. To me. Your name built us a blue hut with white light that wavers, with red at the edges and a green dot. Music. There's a lot I wouldn't have had if you hadn't read to me, says the child, just forget about Kafka. The child's ashamed when I'm ashamed about all this. You're addicted, it says.

Healed by the name of the one you love, you wrote. The one. The right one. Shame, as a child, not to feel every word right when it was praying, that meant in the Our Father loving without any ifs and buts. When it tried, didn't it break down at the word father, trying to love its father? Didn't it always get stuck at father? So never got to the I. By the second word collapsed into despair, because it doesn't work out with him, with the world, love, prayer, feelings, representation of things by words that exist, that it turns out it's not worthy to enter under your roof, and to live under his breast, the heart, the rabbit heart, to live inside oneself, speak but the word, the prayer goes on, and I will be healed. I wanted you to name my name when you make love to me, gently, looking in my eyes as you say it, or scream it, preferably in a

das Kind wartet und kann nicht schlafen die ganze Nacht, und die Mutter schläft. Ich habe keine Weise ausgelassen zu schlafen, als es mich brauchte, genug, um ein ganzes Hochhaus voll mit Müttern in den Schamtod zu schicken. Ich schäme mich so sehr, so oft nicht da gewesen zu sein, mich von dir ernährt zu haben, vom eigenen Kind. Ausserdem hab ich dir Kafka vorgelesen. Bin nachts unter dein Bett gekrochen und habe deine Schätze geplündert, die Schokoladeneier. Ich habe dich so oft vermisst und es nicht zugegeben, mich abgeseilt und dich allein gelassen, gegen mich selbst, ich weiss nicht, ob ich weiter leben kann. Du sagst, dir gefällt dein Name. Du bist mit diesem Namen gekommen. Zu mir. Dein Name hat uns eine blaue Hütte gebaut mit weissem Licht, das wandert, mit Rot an den Rändern und Tupfen Grün. Grün steht für Musik. Ich hätte vieles nicht, wenn du mir nicht vorgelesen hättest, sagt das Kind, lass mal stecken mit Kafka. Es schämt sich, wenn ich mich dafür schäme. Du bist süchtig, sagt es.

Healed by the name of the one you love, you wrote. The one. Der Richtige. Die Richtige. Scham, als Kind, nicht jedes Wort richtig zu fühlen beim Beten, hiesse, beim Vaterunser ohne Wenn und Aber liebend. Ist es nicht beim Versuch, bei Vater wirklich Vater zu lieben, gescheitert? Nicht immer schon bei Vater hängen geblieben? Deshalb gar nicht zu einem Ich gekommen? Beim zweiten Wort in die Verzweiflung gekippt, dass es nicht klappt mit ihm, der Welt, der Liebe, dem Beten, Fühlen, Vertreten der Dinge durch Wörter, die es gibt, dass es nicht würdig ist, einzugehen, unter dein Dach, und damit in

213

church, at a registry office, I don't see you, I thought you were lost already and I hear my name roaring, on Elba. Should I be ashamed of the size of the scream that's needed to bring me into the world? Should I be ashamed of the size of the love without which this scream cannot be brought into the world? Ashamed of its impossibility? But I must have gotten here somehow or other. Isn't it smaller? This is not the subject. There is no subject. This is the subject.

I might have been able to be healed by the name of the man I love. Is the name healable? I am ashamed of your name. Is that right? I blame your name. Your name is divisible. Were all the obstacles in the outer world and we embraced like // *Schiller's* // millions? // *Did this kiss go kiss all the world?* // Weren't we there any more? You don't know how you're supposed to come out of the distance and get in touch, you say later, I'm not supposed to call you. And if I am your appeal? Am I supposed to quit. I quit.

Our wills have a problem. I blame myself for not loving your name in the right way, that I quarrel with it. That I conceal it. Peter and Paul is a cover name. Marcus Aurelius is a cover name. Rainer Maria a cover name. Marie Antoinette a cover name. Will I cover you? Cover you up. Acknowledge, they say. Heal. Capsize? I can't produce you when I'm hiding you at the same time. I can't welcome you if at the same time I'm supposed to be keeping my distance. I can't let you into my life if I have to let you go because you have to be free in order to love me. But I can do all of that

sich selbst, unter seine Brust, das Herz, das Hasenherz, in sich einzuwohnen, sprich nur ein Wort, heisst es weiter, und ich bin geheilt. Ich habe mir gewünscht, dass du meinen Namen nennst, wenn du mich liebst, leise, du dabei in meine Augen siehst, oder schreist, am liebsten in einer Kirche, von einer Kanzel, ich sehe dich nicht, ich glaubte dich schon verloren und höre meinen Namen brüllen, auf Elba. Schäm ich mich für das Ausmass des Schreis, das nötig ist, mich in die Welt zu bringen? Schäm ich mich für das Ausmass der Liebe, ohne die dieser Schrei nicht in die Welt zu bringen ist? Für seine Unmöglichkeit? Ich muss doch irgendwie hier hingekommen sein. Geht es nicht kleiner? Darum geht es nicht. Es geht nicht. Darum geht's.

Ich hätte durch den Namen des Mannes, den ich liebe, geheilt werden können. Ist der Name heilbar? Ich schäme mich für deinen Namen. Stimmt das? Ich gebe deinem Namen die Schuld. Dein Name ist teilbar. Lagen alle Hindernisse in der äusserlichen Welt und wir umschlungen wie Millionen? Waren wir nicht mehr da? Du weisst nicht, wie du aus der Entfernung in die Mitteilung kommen sollst, sagst du später, ich soll dich nicht anrufen. Und wenn ich deine Anrufung bin? Soll ich aufhören. Ich höre auf.

Unsere Willen haben ein Problem. Ich gebe mir die Schuld, dass ich deinen Namen nicht richtig liebe, dass ich hadere mit ihm. Dass ich ihn verdecke. Peter und Paul ist Deckname. Marc Aurel ist Deckname. Rainer Maria ist Deckname. Marie Antoinette ist Deckname. Will ich dich decken? Dich

anyhow when I love you, if you let me love you. You have given me instructions which would have torn apart anybody but me. I was made for things like that, happy about the easiness of the impossible, about the acceleration, timelessness on this road. The skillful act.

I have names for you. Using them, I have never pronounced your own. Robert was the name of the teacher who carved Virgin Marys and hid his head in my lap, so his father wouldn't see him, who was after his wife and his daughter. When I finally touched you, your back, you said: I am no one any more, then you said: I hope we don't disappoint each other, that was weird, since you had left me and didn't want to talk with me: You talked with me, you said, when I touched you.

Is touching the back saying your name? Is touching the back a birth, a baptism? I don't want you, you said, because I flow with you. I put you to the test. There it is again, the flowing, and my instinct of self-preservation against it. The soul is afraid to become wet, says Heraclitus, because this relief can also be your death. *Healed by the love of the one who loves you.* The name. The right man. The right woman. I am ashamed that I didn't heal your name, my love was too small, it is so big that I disappear in it. Disappearing is not good in love. Your name is a promise and a betrayal, an ecclesiastical matter, a holy confusion, spontaneous bewilderment, your name is a great unreciprocated love, and the revenge for it goes right through and through you,

aufdecken. Erkennen, sagen sie. Heilen. Kentern? Ich kann dich nicht holen, wenn ich dich verstecken soll. Ich kann dich nicht aufnehmen, wenn ich mich von dir entfernen soll. Ich kann dich nicht in mein Leben lassen, wenn ich dich verlassen soll dabei, weil du frei sein musst, um mich zu lieben. Das alles aber kann ich, wenn ich dich liebe, wenn du mich dich lieben lässt. Du hast mir Aufträge gegeben, die eine andere als mich sofort zerrissen hätten. Ich war dafür gemacht, glücklich über die Leichtigkeit des Unmöglichen, über die Beschleunigung, Zeitlosigkeit auf dieser Bahn. Der kunstvolle Akt.

Ich habe Namen für dich. Deinen habe ich nie ausgesprochen dabei. Robert hiess der Lehrer, der Marien schnitzte und seinen Kopf in meinem Schoss versteckte, damit sein Vater ihn nicht sieht, der seiner Frau und seiner Tochter nachstellte. Als ich dich zuletzt berührte, deinen Rücken, hast du gesagt: Ich bin niemand mehr, dann hast du gesagt: Hoffentlich enttäuschen wir uns nicht, das war bizarr, denn du hattest mich verlassen und wolltest nicht mit mir reden: Du redest ja mit mir, hast du gesagt, als ich dich berührte.

Ist den Rücken berühren den Namen sagen? Ist den Rücken berühren Geburt, eine Taufe? Ich will dich nicht, sagst du, weil ich mit dir fliesse. Ich habe dich auf die Probe gestellt. Da ist es wieder, das Fliessen, und mein Lebenserhaltungtrieb dagegen. Die Seele fürchtet die Feuchtigkeit, weil diese ihre Erleichterung, aber auch ihr Tod sein kann, ach Heraklit. Healed by the love of the one who loves you. Der Name. Der

and through me. Can you love it out of me, as big as the love from your mother to your father, and vice versa? Not vice versa. From Peter to Paul. From Saul to Paul. From the back of the horse under his hooves. From marrow to aura. From Mary to Magdalene, who anointed your feet, to the madeleine that cradled your memories in your lap. From disaster to the stars. You are secure in me, you know that, and nothing happens to you.Nothing happened to your father in Maria too.

I'm fed up with it. Then tore you in two. There are upleapings in you. Goat trance. Murky cup. Soft flannel, green, yours, that I set fire to at year's end, over the Thames. I'd rather burn all the houses, streets, lamps, ships than you. You are not of this world. Over you the skies change, the stars are hooves, that's how it is with you. Your name at first glance is a curse. At the second, suicide. At the third, a riddle. At the fourth and for our Guardian Angels your name is a gateway to you, and I'm ashamed, I never said it, never, only when I stroked your back, softly to your vertebrae, but never out loud, never, when your face was turned to me, never did I say Peter and Paul to you in this love of ours, never Marcus, never Aurelius, never Antoinette and not Robert. From here on your way goes on, you said, as you screamed my name, I had to overhear that, otherwise I would have turned sick, Poo, tender loved Pook.

Love, the word, when that falls, it is finished, is that so? No. I am ashamed for coming so late. That's it. The ugliness. The

Richtige. Die Richtige. Ich schäme mich, dass ich deinen Namen nicht heilte, meine Liebe zu klein war, die so gross ist, dass ich in ihr verschwinde. Verschwinden ist nicht gut in der Liebe. Dein Name ist ein Versprechen und ein Verrat, eine Kirchenangelegenheit, heilige Konfusion, spontane Verwirrung, dein Name ist eine grosse unerwiderte Liebe, und die Rache dafür mitten durch dich durch und durch mich. Kannst du es aus mir herauslieben, die Grösse der Liebe deiner Mutter zu deinem Vater, und umgekehrt? Umgekehrt nicht. Von Peter zu Paul. Von Saulus zu Paulus. Vom Rücken des Pferdes unter seine Hufe. Vom Mark zur Aura. Von Maria zu Magdalena, die deine Füsse salbt, zur Madelaine, die deine Erinnerung in ihrem Schoss wiegt. Vom Desaster zu den Sternen. Du bist in mir sicher, das weisst du, und es passiert dir nichts. Auch deinem Vater ist in Maria nichts passiert.

Ich bin es leid. Dann reiss dich halt entzwei. Es gibt Sprünge in dir. Ziegentrance. Trübe Tasse. Waschlappen, grüner, deiner, den ich Silvester über der Themse verbrenne. Eher brennen die Häuser, Strassen, Laternen, Schiffe als du. Du bist nicht von dieser Welt. Über dir wechselt der Himmel, die Sterne sind Hufe, das ist so mit dir. Dein Name ist auf den ersten Blick Fluch. Auf den zweiten Selbstmord. Auf den dritten Rätsel. Auf den vierten und für unsere Schutzengel ist dein Name das Tor zu dir, und ich schäme mich, ihn nicht, und zwar niemals, nur, wenn ich deinen Rücken berührte, leise zu deinen Wirbeln, aber nie laut, nie, als dein Gesicht mir zugewandt war, nie habe ich Peter und Paul zu dir gesagt in dieser Liebe dabei, nie Marc, nie Aurel, nie Antoinette und

deafness. The delays. Fragments of seconds are involved. If I had been spontaneous, I would have died with happiness. I had passed my rightful death already when I was three months old. *Healed by the healing of the name of the one whom you love and who loves you.* Love. The right one. I was blocked. You tried it. You did not come through. Come with me, you said. You had no patience. It had to be right away, the way we are right away. How could I come into the world without it. Love. It went without. Stupid way of running a planet. Am I in the world? I have not come into the world, shame has gone ahead, shame is juicy and nourishes my shadow. Which raises the rifle and spits ink.

And now to the Mothers
PROMISED POP SONG NUMBER FOUR

To the stones
I have to go
through the crocodiles
through the back
yours, mine

nicht Robert. Von hier an geht dein Weg weiter, hast du gesagt, als du meinen dabei schriest, das musste ich überhören, mir wäre sonst übel geworden, Pu, zart liebte Puk.

Liebe, das Wort, wenn das fällt, ist es aus, ist das so? Nein. Ich schäme mich für mein Zuspätkommen. Das ist es. Die Hässlichkeit. Die Taubheit. Die Verschiebung. Es geht um Bruchteile von Sekunden. Wäre ich spontan gewesen, wäre ich vor Glück geplatzt. Ich habe meinen richtigen Tod schon als ich drei Monate alt war verpasst. Healed by the healing of the name of the one whom you love and who loves you. Die Liebe. Die Richtige. Ich war verstopft. Du hast es versucht. Du bist nicht durchgedrungen. Kommst du mit, hast du gesagt. Du hattest keine Zeit. Es sollte so sofort sein, wie wir sofort sind. Wie konnte ich ohne sie auf die Welt kommen. Die Liebe. Es ist ohne gegangen. Dummes Erdsystem. Bin ich auf der Welt? Ich bin nicht auf die Welt gekommen, die Scham ist vorausgegangen, sie ist saftig und nährt meinen Schatten. Der streckt die Flinte und spuckt Tinte.

Und jetzt zu den Müttern
PROMISED POP SONG NUMBER FOUR

Zu den Steinen
muss ich
durch die Krokodile
durch den Rücken
deinen, meinen

the one I buzz around
with hands, yours
mine, twigs, fingers
berries, fingertips through the pictures
love worlds, they disentangle us
"Freedom and Obedience" you say, even
when I am bound, you belong to me, on me and on top of me
to break, escape, disentangle
lizards, chameleons, orchids, all mixed up
flow, golden from you, buzzing
out of the cartilage archive, gingerbread house
sinister forests grind me against you, carve
out of my legs the posts I'm bound to, moldy lichens
rejected cheeks, stains

To the gold
I have to go through hell
this pharyngeal cavity of aged beasts
through sorrows go natural
through the kidneys, and all these
loin-hugging entrances – wide open to life
creaking hinges, skirmishes, damnable
dead end streets, treadmills, Sisyphus
marries a hamster, wheels and stones
and mountains, omnipotent dwarves
for the ancient teeth of the great mothers
for poison in the angles of the mouths of adders
under the water I have to
go to the stones

den ich uns umschwirre
mit den Händen, deinen
meinen, Äste, Finger
Beeren, Kuppen durch die Bilder
Liebeswelten, die sich uns entflechten
«Freiheit und Gehorsam» sagst du, auch
wenn ich gefesselt bin, gehörst du mir, auf mir und über mir
brechen, ausbrechen, entwirren
Echsen, Chamäleon, Orchideen, verwechseln
fliessen, golden aus dir, schwirren
aus den Knorpelarchiven, Knusperhäuschen
bösen Wäldern mich dir entgegendrechseln
aus den Beinen, den gebundenen Pfosten, Schimmelflechten
ausschlagenden Backen, den Flecken

Zu dem Gold
muss ich durch die Hölle
diese Rachenhöhle alter Tiere
durch die Schmerzen geh natürlich
durch die Nieren, und all diese
lendennahen Türen – lebensweiten
knarrenden Scharniere, Scharmützel, vermaledeiten
Sackgassen, Tretmühlen, vermählen
Hamster und Sisyphus, Räder und Steine
und Berge, omnipotente Zwerge
zu den alten Zähnen der grossen Mütter
zum Gift in den Ecken der Münder der Nattern
unter das Wasser muss ich
zu den Steinen

223

bat that I am, giant bird beast
imploring, fluttering
like fear two wings
and tricks me under the toads
still under there under the sparks drunk on blackberries
of the under down there under, same time I breathe upwards
climb
as if in heaven above
only right the stones lived

firmament is word for limit
but there is none
there's a transmitter
a trance mother
translators, Styx experts, loving
embodiments and what holds them

To the middle I must go by sword, the
heavy, the slashed in two cut through the
body that is desperate when it
is not held, burdened
no current, through it the current doesn't
flow, the slashed apart is
when and how he misses
missing misses the yard long
misery stretch between heaven/hell
long, and tears apart and forgets
that this is the body, the one
he misses, the death wood, through

ich Fledermaus, ich Riesenvogelvieh
flehen, flattern
als sei die Angst zwei Flügel
und trüge mich unter die Unken
noch drunter unter die brombeerbetrunkenen Funken
der unteren drunten, gleichzeitig atme ich oben
steige
als ob im Himmel droben
erst recht die Steine wohnten

Firmament ist Wort für Grenze
doch es gibt sie nicht
es gibt Transmitter
Trancemütter
Übersetzer, Styxexperten, liebende
Verkörperungen und ihre Behälter

Zu der Mitte muss ich durch das Schwert, das
Schwere, das entzweischlägt mitten durch den
Körper, der verzweifelt, wenn er
nicht gehalten ist, geladen
stromlos, durch den der Strom nicht
fliesst, der entzweigeschlagen ist
wenn und wie er sich vermisst
das Vermissen misst die ellenlange
Elendsstrecke zwischen Himmel/Hölle
lang, und zerreisst und vergisst
dass dies der Körper ist, den er
vermisst, das Totenholz, durch

the stones the gold flows impure
if you are the gold as in hard
times stone
when he brings you

Stay metal
gleam silver
silver gleams, bright and
adder nip poisonous
tongue quiver quick and you
make yourself from fields
from the blood ground
when it strikes stones again
then through the stroke
the world strikes
coils flickers its tongue
in you
unscheduled
who endures it
the bright pavilion

SCHAM 16

Ich schäme mich für Sprache.

Ich schäme mich für meine Haut.

Aber das Gefühl der Haut gibt Energie. Kopf des Drachen im
ersten Haus, heisst, die Energie kommt von Haut, vom Wetter,

die Steine fliesst das Gold unhold
wenn du das Gold bist wie in harten
Zeiten Stein
wenn er dich holt

Stay metal
glänz silbern
silbern glänzt, hell und
natternprisengiftig
zungenvibrationenschnell und du dich
vom Acker machst
vom Blutgrund
wenn es wieder Steine schlägt
denn durch den Schlag
schlägt sich die Welt
schlängelt, züngelt sich
in dir
unbestellt
wer das aushält
das helle Zelt

SHAME 16

I am ashamed of language

I am ashamed of my skin

but the feeling of the skin gives energy. Head of the Dragon
in the first house means energy comes from skin, from the

vom Kontakt des Anderen mit dem Körper des Selbst. Das heisst Haut. Ich schäme mich, wieviel meine Haut fühlt.

Scham ist Energie.

Mit einer schnellen Bewegung zog sie ihre Bluse aus und ich schämte mich, ich rannte aus dem Raum und wankte zum Swimmingpool, konnte kaum atmen. Scham ist das Gegenteil von Atem. Ich hörte sie über mich lachen, als ich am Fenster des Raums vorbeiging, aus dem ich mich gerade geflüchtet hatte. Ich war elf. Ich schämte mich. Die Frauen lachten über den Jungen, der dachte, sie würden sich ausziehen. Ich schämte mich und studierte das Wasser im Pool, seine Kräusel schienen blau und golden, doch ich wusste, das Wasser hat keine Farbe.

Nichts hat eine Farbe.

Das Wasser hatte keine Farbe, ich wusste das, das wunderbare Blau war von der kreidigen alten Farbe auf den Schwimmbadwänden, die gar nicht schön aussah, wenn das Schwimmbad entwässert war. Das Gold kam von der späten Abendsonne, die schräg über den Hügel schlenderte, der uns von der Stadt abschirmte, der Hügel, auf dem das Wild nun spazierte, entspannt, wie Gott in Eden.

Gan Eden.
Der Katechismus.
Warum machte Er dich? Um ihn zu lieben und ihm zu dienen

weather, from the contact of the other with the body of the self. That means skin. I am ashamed of how much my skin feels.

Shame is energy.

She pulled off her blouse in one quick movement and I was ashamed, I ran out of the room and walked by the swimming pool not able to breathe. Shame is the opposite of breath. I heard them laughing at me as I passed the window of the room I had just fled. I was eleven. I was ashamed. The women were laughing at the boy who thought they were getting undressed. I was ashamed and I studied the water in the pool, its ripples seemed blue and golden, but I knew that the water has no color.

Nothing has any color.

The water had no color, I knew that, the beautiful blue was from the chalky old paint on the walls of the pool that didn't look at all beautiful when the pool was drained. The gold was from the late afternoon sun slanting over the hill that hid us from town, the hill where the deer were walking now, relaxed, like God in Eden.

Gan Eden.
The catechism.
Why did He make you? To love him and serve him and to be happy with him in this world and the next.

und mit ihm glücklich zu sein in dieser Welt und der nächsten. Ich schäme mich für die nächste Welt, wie nah sie ist.

Ich schäme mich für die Farben, wie sehr ich sie will.

Die Primärfarben: Rot, der Heilige Geist. Gelb, der Sohn, der Sein Licht über uns bringt. Blau, der Vater, der dunkle Himmel, das Ungesehene, Boehmes Ungrund, der Schlund über uns.

Gott ist der Schlund am Grund, auf dem wir leben.

Die Farben sind natürlich die Dreieinigkeit.

Ich schäme mich für Gott. Gott zu wollen. Gott ist lächerlich. Nein, Religion ist lächerlich, Gott ist auf der anderen Seite.

Gott ist die grösste Scham, der grösste Skandal.

So las ich Edgar Allan Poe, der sagte: *Irrer, wir legten sie lebend in die Gruft!*

Er schämte sich für seine Schwester. Sie war eine Aussätzige oder so. Sie kam zurück an seine Tür. Der Aussätzige kommt immer wieder nach Hause. Freud nennt das die Rückkehr des Unterdrückten. Es ist in Wahrheit die einzige Geschichte in der Weltliteratur, ob sie Odysseus heisst oder Sindbad oder Marco Polo oder Madeleine Usher, das Unterdrückte kommt immer zurück.

I am ashamed of the next world, how close it is.

I am ashamed of colors, of wanting them so much.

The primary colors: Red, the Holy Spirit. Yellow, the Son who brings His light among us. Blue, the Father, the dark of sky, the unseen, Boehme's Ungrund, the abyss above us.

God is the abyss at the bottom of which we live.

The colors are the Trinity of course.

I am ashamed of God. Wanting God. God is so ridiculous. No, religion is ridiculous, God is on the other side.

God is the biggest shame, the biggest scandal.

So I read Edgar Allan Poe and it said: *Madman, we have put her, living, in the tomb!*

He was ashamed of his sister. She was a leper or something like that. She came back to his door. The leper always comes home. Freud calls this the Return of the Repressed. It is in fact the only story in world literature, whether it's called Odysseus or Sindbad or Marco Polo or Madeleine Usher, the repressed always comes back.

I am ashamed of my leprosy. I wrote a story: *Comment je suis devenu lépreux.* It told the truth.

Ich schäme mich für meine Lepra. Ich schrieb eine Geschichte: *Comment je suis devenu lépreux.* Sie sagte die Wahrheit.

Ich schäme mich für Worte wie: Wahrheit, Lüge, Gott, unterdrückt. Ich schäme mich für Worte wie: Geschichte, zurück, Rücken, sagen. Ich schäme mich für Worte wie: kommen und gehen und sein und schlafen und wachen. Niemand von uns weiss, was sie heissen. Was heisst kommen?

Es heisst so viel, dass es nichts heisst. Meinen. Ich schäme mich, so viele Dinge zu meinen. Wenn ich ein Wort wäre, würde ich so viele Dinge bedeuten, dass die Leute mich niemals benutzen würden. Oder die ganze Zeit. Ich will das der/die/das sein. *The.* Ich schäme mich *the* sein zu wollen. Aber *the* ist das einzige, was du sein kannst. *The* ist nah am Meer. *The* lebt in einem ruhigen Park nah am Zoo. *The* kann die Löwen vor ihrem Frühstück brüllen hören. *The* kann selbst die Fische ihre Gebete flüstern hören. Fische beten zum Salz.

Ich schäme mich, so viel zu beten. Ich denke: Alles, was ich tue, ist ein Gebet, alles, was ich sage, ist ein Psalm. Ich schäme mich für Psalme.

Ein Psalm will nur in deinem Schoss liegen, seinen Kopf in dich vergraben und Hosianna schreien. Dinge wollen so viele Dinge.

Dinge wollen tun und sein. Ich schäme mich fürs Wollen.

I am ashamed of words like truth, lie, God, repressed. I am ashamed of words like story, back, tell. I am ashamed of words like come and go and be and sleep and wake. None of us knows what they mean. What does come mean?

It means so much it means nothing. I am ashamed of meaning so many things. If I were a word I would mean so many things that people would never use me at all. Or use me all the time. I want to be the. I am ashamed of wanting to be the. But the is the only thing to be. The is near the sea. The lives in a quiet park near the zoo. The can hear the lions roaring before their breakfast. The can even hear the fish whispering their prayers. Fish pray to salt.

I am ashamed of praying so much. I think: everything I do is a prayer, everything I say is a psalm. I am ashamed of psalms.

A psalm only wants to lie in your lap, burrow into you and cry Hosannah. Things want so many things.

Things want to do and want to be. I am ashamed of wanting.

The disease she had, Madeleine, whose name is the French memory of Magdalena, Maria Magdalena (which was Dietrich's baptismal name), Magdalena, who was Jesus's friend, his very dear, dear friend, and who was the first to see him after he woke up, Magdalene, a revised harlot, a

Die Krankheit, die sie hatte, Madeleine, deren Name das französische Gedächtnis von Magdalena ist, Maria Magdalena (was Dietrichs Taufname war), Magdalena, die Jesus Freund war, sein sehr sehr teurer Freund, die erste, die ihn sah, nachdem er aufwachte, Magdalena, eine revidierte Hure, eine transponierte Prostituierte, sagen sie. Ich schäme mich für das, was sie sagen. Egal, Madeleine, all diese Namen und Schatten, Madeleine war seine Schwester. Sie hatte eine Krankheit, Auszehrung. Was könnte das sein ausser Lepra? Aussatz, die schwärende Wunde, die auch der Aus-Satz ist, Aus, *das Urteil*, Exil und Verbannung, die Krankheit, die dir das Aus sagt, es ist aus, dich ausspuckt aus dem Satz.

Könnte es sein, dass die berühmte Lepra aus dem Mittelalter im neunzehnten Jahrhundert zu der Krankheit wurde, die wir Liebe nennen? Die fatale Krankheit, die einen Mann von seinen Freunden verbannt und ihn in die Wildnis treibt, wo nur ein Ziel ständig vor ihm steht, die Geliebte, Medizin für die Liebe, die heilende Andere, *die ferne Geliebte, Heiland*, Heilung, Hilfe? Nur sie. Nur sie für nur ihn.

Dann kriegten auch die Frauen die Krankheit. Nur er für nur sie. Und eine Frau wurde von ihrer Familie und von Gott verbannt und schmachtete hinweg wegen ihm.

Sie war in ihren Bruder verliebt. Er war in sie verliebt. Sie kam immer auf ihn zu. Das war die Art ihrer Krankheit. Er unterdrückte sie. Er dürstete nach ihr und konnte seinen Durst nicht aushalten. Weil sie lebendig war, legte er sie in

prostitute transposed, they say. I am ashamed of what they say. Anyhow, Madeleine, all those names and shadows, Madeleine was his sister. She had a disease, a wasting disease. What could that be but leprosy? Aussatz, the running sore, which is also the out-sentence, das Urteil of exile and banishment, the disease that says you out, spits you out of the sentence.

Could it be that this famous mediaeval leprosy became in the nineteenth century the disease that was called Love? The fatal disease that banishes a man from his friends and drives him out into the wilderness where only one goal is steadily before him, the beloved, the cure for love, the healing other, die ferne Geliebte, Heiland, healing, help? Only her. Only her for only him.

Then women caught the disease too. Only him for only her. And a woman was banished from her family and God, and pined away for him.

She was in love with her brother. He was in love with her. She kept coming towards him. That was the nature of her disease. He repressed her. He lusted for her and could not endure his lust. Because she was alive, he put her in the tomb. Don't you mean Although she was alive …? No. If she had been dead, if desire was dead, if nothing moved the burning sister towards her combustible brother, no need to bury her.

die Gruft. Meinst du nicht, obwohl sie lebendig war? Nein. Wenn sie tot gewesen wäre, wenn das Verlangen tot gewesen wäre, wenn nichts die liebende Schwester in Richtung erregbaren Bruder bewegt hätte, gäbe es keinen Grund, sie zu beerdigen.

So ist die Gesellschaft. Wir beerdigen nur die Lebendigen.

Also legte er sie in die Gruft, aber sie wollte dort nicht bleiben. Sie wollte nicht tot bleiben, und er hörte ihre Sehnsucht. *Sehnsucht singt.* Er hört sie überall, in jedem Ton, den ein altes Haus macht, er hört sie kommen und kommen, hört ihre Verzückungen einzigartiger beschämender Hingabe, hört durch die Wände und Tapeten gedämpft ihre Schreie, während er sich beschämt misshandelt dafür, an sie zu denken. Und es wird immer lauter, während sie immer weiter kommt.

Die Magdalene, die Madeleine, ist das Gedächtnis, das immer zurück kommt, er kann es nicht unterdrücken, Irrer, er schreit Richtung Freund, doch in Wirklichkeit zu sich selbst, Irrer, irre, zu denken, ich könnte ihre Hingabe bannen, ihre Krankheit, die all ihre Trennung verschwendet ins Sehnen nach mir, banne mein Sehnen. Irrer, sie ist an der Tür.

Und mit einem gellenden Schrei fällt der Irre, und das Haus fällt mit ihm. Eine berühmte Geschichte.

Ich schäme mich für Türen.

This is society. We bury only the living.

So he put her in the tomb but she wouldn't stay there. She wouldn't stay dead and he heard her longing. Sehnsucht singt. He hears her everywhere, in every sound an old house makes, he hears her coming and coming, hears her raptures of solitary shameful devotion, hears her cries muffled through the walls and tapestries as he shamefully abuses himself thinking of her. And the noises never stop, they get louder as she keeps coming.

The Magdalene, the Madeleine, is the memory that keeps coming back, he cannot repress her, madman, he cries to his friend but really to himself, madman, mad to think I could banish her devotion, her sickness that wastes all her separation into yearning for me, banish my yearning, madman, she is at the door!

And with a shriek the madman falls and the house falls with him. A famous story.

I am ashamed of doors.

Passages by RK written in German and not otherwise translated.

2.5 I am a shame. Shame means *Scham*, though sham means false. I am false.
Shame and Guilt, you have to distinguish them, no, you have to decide.

6.45 I am the spirit that always negates. (Mephistopheles says this in Goethe's
Faust.)

8.71 Missile silos
  73 bread rolls
  79 the oldest song
    and ever the distances shimmer blue
  85 I am the flag, and I am the only one, and I am enough
  87 Genickschuss = coup de grace

10.111 Philosophy is difficult, the woman says
    Philosophy is thought without thinking, is a poem without poetry, a
    song without music. A Grecian fountain from which no more water
    flows.
   123 (*Wollust* in German means lust, while *Lust* in German means pleasure
    or delight.)

12. 137 but always false. I am always ashamed of being anywhere, anywhere at
all, anywhere out of the world, as Baudelaire saw it, and here the bridges leaps
over the Danube like the fire that comes to kiss the dry fields of rye […] the
soldiers are dead and their once turkey-red flowers withered a hundred years
[…] down to the fairgrounds and there they could touch the girls
   139 mere form. […] But also pure, like a reminiscence that a man or a child
is able to hold in his hand till his clever skin shall have finished its investigation,
[…] mucus membrane, the text explains […] farewell, my handsome officer of
the Guards […] all her screaming and complaining […] the song is over
   141 tender, exciting
    Sentences. What is a sentence?
   143 Coccyx. Clavicle.
   145 Nobody's bone
    Linden tree.
    The sea. Neuter.

13.188

Ah Rilke I love a lot
Robert's alternative Pop Song to counter Birgit's Pop Song
Number three

Ah Rainer René Renée
I love you a lot
you discovered
yes, no, you invented
the intersexual language
with which the Angels
of the *Hadith* speak
and speak with us
the sorry glory
of some old story
religion religion

Santa Maria Formosa
I knelt down
I prayed
to Saint Lucia
on account of my eyes

and the angels there
what do they hear now
after so much poetry
they still talk
they caress
my vulnerable earskin
I am afraid
o Renée René Rainer
Renatus Renata
what a girl you are!
I am afraid
of your gold and ivory
with emeralds with breast milk
with gondolas
you compel

the dead cat sings
the burnt church
melts, it fills up with eyewax
with priestly seed with nard
candles lemons wine
of course wine
you compel you compel

I hear you I want to
read you
you are never ever ashamed
always gracile and unconditioned and richly poor
never jamais and fresh nowheres
dream steam from ocean liner
women
every soul is a woman
in you every word a shame
you are never ashamed
to unenchant me.

_____

16. 235   *Aussatz* = leprosy
         die ferne Geliebte = the distant beloved (a Beethoven song-cycle)